School Learning: Mechanisms and Processes

Psychology and Education

General Editor: Gerald Cortis

Child Development
Geoffrey Brown

The Social Context of Teaching
Gerald Cortis

Personality and Education
David Fontana

Learning and Behaviour Difficulties in School
D. J. Leach and E. C. Raybould

School Learning: Mechanisms and Processes
R. J. Riding

School Learning:
Mechanisms and Processes

R. J. Riding

Open Books
London

First published 1977 by Open Books Publishing Ltd
21 Tower Street, London WC2H 9NS

© R. J. Riding 1977

Hardback: ISBN 0 7291 0066 9

Paperback: ISBN 0 7291 0061 8

Filmset in 10pt Linotron Imprint

Printed by T. & A. Constable Ltd
Hopetoun Street, Edinburgh

Contents

To Patricia,
Adrian, Alison and Julia

Editor's introduction

How do children learn? Richard Riding's book begins by looking at the psychological factors in children's learning and goes on to discuss various types of learning and the psychological processes associated with them. Attention is paid to the important topic of remembering what has been learned, and the processes of reasoning and problem solving are examined to see under what conditions pupils will be able to think effectively. Regrettably teaching and learning are not necessarily related, since it is the learner's psychological mechanisms that primarily determine the nature of what is learnt and/or retained rather than the act of teaching itself. Hence how teachers might plan and evaluate their pupils' learning, in the light of these facts, is reviewed, as is recent research on individual styles of learning. A feature of the text is the discussion points at the end of each chapter.

School Learning: Mechanisms and Processes is one of the titles in the *Psychology and Education* series. Though consumer preference does not constitute the sole criterion of selecting topics for course design, such a preference is a demand that both authors and publishers have not usually been able to meet with exactitude, since reliable information about demand has not been readily available until now. The selection of titles in this series was based on the results of an extensive nationwide survey of teachers of educational studies on the staffs of polytechnics and colleges that I carried out in 1973. The five titles represent the areas that teachers in higher education rated as the most essential elements in their actual or proposed courses in the psychological area of education. The authors, who have all had extensive teaching experience themselves, have taken as their principal aim the introduction of important psychological concepts in each area that are relevant to both educational theory and practice. Our purpose has been to write simply and clearly so that key areas are revealed and a framework is provided on which a student can build further knowledge. The framework embraces both new and long-standing concepts, since new knowledge has a relation to time past. The unity in the series arises from the ultimate selection of the five titles (in terms of the highest survey ratings) by the consumers themselves, though each title has been designed to stand on its own. Given the hybrid nature of both psychology and education some minor overlap of topic areas is inevitable and, in many ways, welcome.

References in the text to the work of other writers, e.g., Jones (1975) are provided so that students may be encouraged, where appropriate to follow up the source named. The book or article so quoted will be listed in the References (which also double as a Name Index) at the back of the book.

Gerald Cortis

1

Introduction

Some basic questions

Why do children attend school? The simple answer to this question is *to learn*. This, in turn, leads to two further basic queries; how do pupils learn, and what should they learn?

Consider a practical situation. A group of primary school children is doing a topic on canals. They are learning by listening to what their teacher has to say, by reading in books and articles, by seeing a film about canals in other countries. by visiting a local canal system and going on a trip on a barge, and by constructing a model canal. These are the activities the pupils engage in during the topic, but how do they learn? Basically, learning is receiving the information they see, hear and feel, into their minds and adding it to what they already know.

What should pupils learn? Consider the categories of learning that occurred in connection with the topic. The most obvious is the reception of *information* about canals, about how they were built, what they were used for and how they can be utilised now. In addition, the children learned *strategies* of how to find out, how to express themselves, how to look things up, how to observe, how to plan the stages of the construction of a model. They also acquired *motor skills* from their model making and drawing, how to control their hands and fingers to shape and mould, and to control a pencil and rule. They were involved in the *social learning* of how to get on with one another, how to be thoughtful towards one another, and of the values of the society

1

in which they live. The range of learning that takes place is wide.

We have looked at what the pupils can learn. What they should learn will be determined by the aims and values of the society in which they live. A child brought up within a primitive tribe in a jungle in South America may be taught how to make and use a blow-pipe for hunting wild animals. In an industrial society a child would be more likely to be taught how to programme a computer. Psychology is neutral in that it describes the varieties of learning that can take place. The choice of what is learned rests with the teacher and society.

The human learning system   What is the capital city of France? How do you make a cup of tea? What is your name? You didn't find any difficulty in answering these questions. Where did the information come from? You had it stored in your *memory*. You were not conscious of the information until you read the questions which directed you to search and retrieve the items. Have you any other information in memory? Yes, lots and lots, and you can recall it when you need it.

How did all that information get into your memory? You learned it from what you were told, saw, read and experienced in other ways. As you received the material you were conscious of it and you analysed what it meant in what we will call *short-term memory*, and then transferred the meaning into your large memory store. How did you analyse the information? It was in terms of its meaning, which you determined from what you already know. When you read a sentence like, 'The children went into the park and ran to a slide to play', you analyse each word and work out the meaning of the whole sentence.

How does the information get into short-term memory? Through your senses. You see, you hear, you feel. Light comes from objects, like the page of this book, and enters the lens in the front of your eye and is focussed on the light sensitive layer inside the rear of the eye, which transmits the image to the short-term memory. Sound is carried by the air to your ears which pick up the vibrations and transmit the patterns to short-term memory. Your hands feel the texture and shape of objects and this data is also relayed to short-term memory.

There are, then, three stages of the learning system; reception by the senses, analysis of the meaning by short-term memory, and storage of the information in the large long-term memory.

Understanding   Mr Bull has just finished describing to a class of fourteen-year-olds how they can find the density of an irregularly shaped piece of material. He now gives each of them a piece of stone and instructs them to find its density. After about fifteen minutes most of the class have worked out a result, but at least half a dozen pupils have done nothing constructive. Mr Bull is very strict and is not to be trifled with, and so it was not for want of trying. Of these children take Tom, for instance. Why is he finding the work difficult? He is a nice lad, rarely naughty, usually fairly quiet. When asked by Mr Bull about his lack of progress he feels awkward and rather fearful, and explains rather hesitatingly that he does not understand how to apply the method. We ask ourselves why he has had difficulty. Obviously he is the sort of pupil who wants to learn. To find the reason for his difficulty we need to go back through the lesson. At the start of the session Tom was attentive and understood what was said. However, as time went by his thoughts began to wander. He could still hear Mr Bull, of course, but he was no longer fully analysing the meaning of what he heard, and so the details of the method were not stored in his long-term memory.

Gillian, another member of the class, had a different problem. She had listened very attentively to Mr Bull, but somehow it just did not make sense to her. She did not find what he said meaningful. The reason for this was simple; she had been absent for a fortnight with flu and had missed the preceding lessons on the topic of density. Consequently this new information could not be understood because the material that was essential to its comprehension was missing from Gillian's memory.

Here we have the two basic reasons why pupils do not understand what they hear or read. They either do not analyse the information properly, or they have not the necessary existing knowledge to give it meaning. Sometimes children do not analyse the material because, like Tom, they dream. Others do not attend because they want to play up. The effect is the same in both cases, they do not understand the lesson. Sometimes pupils cannot comprehend the new information because, like Gillian, they have missed some essential related material through absence. Others may lack the necessary knowledge because they were badly taught or not taught it, or were not attending on a previous occasion. The final effect is the same in all cases, the new information is not learned in a meaningful way. The basic principle of learning is that what we see and hear is understood in terms of what we already know.

Remembering   Have you a good memory? Many people complain that they haven't. Why do we often find that we can't recall what we read last week? There are three possible reasons.

To begin with we may not actually have analysed what we read. We had the book before us, our eyes scanned the words, but our thoughts were elsewhere, and like Tom we did not completely process the meaning of what we read and did not store it in memory. We can only remember what we have actually learned, and so can the children we teach.

Secondly, we may be trying to recall information in a form that is different from that in which we stored it. If you read a novel last week and a friend asks you to say what it was about, you find that your version of it is almost always in your own words and style, and not in the literal wording of the original. When we read or hear something we tend to abstract from it the general meaning, the main sense. Consequently, when you recall something you read last week, if you try to think of the exact words on a page you will be very unlikely to recall them because that is not what you learned and stored.

Finally, perhaps you can't remember because you have difficulty in locating the information in memory. Our memories are probably rather like libraries in which books are arranged on the shelves according to their contents. To find a book you look it up in a catalogue which tells you which shelf it is on. Often you find that you cannot locate a book because it has been placed on the wrong shelf by mistake, and when you look for it you conclude that it isn't there, because you can't find it. This may be why we cannot recall what we have learned, because although it is in memory, we cannot locate it. It may also happen, of course, that information that was learned is lost from memory, or as we would say, forgotten.

In school, remembering what has previously been taught is important, because new learning can only be meaningful if it is understood.

Thinking and reasoning   Why do children learn at school? So that they will be able to cope with life, to earn their living, to enjoy creation and to live life to the full. Should they learn facts or should they learn how to think and to be creative? In times past the emphasis was often on the learning of information. More recently some teachers have arged that thinking and creativity are all important and that learning information is not the thing.

As is usually the case, the ideal lies between these two extremes. A moment's thought about a real-life situation will tell us why. Fred is travelling home late one night on a very quiet country road, when he notices that the little red ignition warning light on his instrument panel is on. He has a problem to solve. Why has it come on? How does he solve it? He searches through his memory of the facts of how the engine works. It is probably because the fan belt has broken, he thinks, and he notices that the thermometer is indicating that the engine is beginning to overheat. This confirms his conclusion because the fan belt drives both the generator and also the pump that circulates the water in the cooling system through the radiator. He stops, he is miles from anywhere. What can he do? The obvious answer would be to fit another fan belt but, as he tells himself, he was silly enough not to carry one. He looks under the bonnet, yes, the fan belt has gone, what can he do? He looks up and his eyes settle on a piece of nylon rope that must have been blown off a lorry, hanging in the hedge. Suddenly he is creative, he cuts a length off the rope, ties it carefully and fits in place of the lost fan belt. It will probably slip a bit but it will get him home.

To cope with this situation Fred needed both the facts he had previously learned about how cars work, and the ability to think creatively to solve his problem. In school, children need to learn the basic information that is useful in life, and also to be encouraged to question and to think critically.

The structure of this book   In the chapters that follow, the processes by which children learn, remember and think will be described. Since children are all different, their personality and learning style will be considered. Finally, the planning of learning sequences will be discussed so that the teacher can make the learning efficient.

2

The basic processes of learning

How do children learn?

What are the processes by which children represent in their minds what they see and hear? Imagine yourself in a room in a school. The class is involved in work on a topic. A child gets up from the table where he is working, comes over to you, and asks a question about his project. You think for a moment and then give four sentences in reply. The child nods and returns to his place. This is an everyday happening which the teacher takes for granted, and yet when we stop to think about this situation, it is quite amazing that ideas in the mind of the teacher can be transferred into the mind of the pupil in this way. How does the transfer take place?

There are two aspects of the reception of new information by a pupil. These are the *stages* of the learning system through which the material is processed, and the types, or *levels*, of analysis that are performed. This distinction may be made clearer by considering a parallel with the tape recorder. Suppose you record a concert — the sound must pass through three *stages*. The first is the microphone which picks up the sound and translates it into electrical pulses. At a second stage these pulses are made stronger, and suitable for recording, by passing them through an amplifier. Finally, the pulses are recorded on the tape in the form of a magnetic trace. Although the analogy is rather crude, and not completely accurate, the same sort of stages apply to human learning. The senses, eyes or ears receive information which they turn into electrical pulses. These go to a part of the brain where they are analysed into forms that are suitable for storing in the memory in another area of the brain.

In addition to thinking of a tape recording as a series of stages, it may also be viewed in terms of the quality, or *level*, of the analysis of the sounds. You have recorded a music concert. If your machine is of a high quality it will accept a wide range of notes and on reproduction will give you something closely resembling the original sound. A poor recorder, on the other hand, will only partially accept the notes and so the playback will sound much less rich than the original music. Again there is a parallel with learning. When you hear a talk or read a book, you may either process the information to a high *level*, so that you have a complete understanding of it, or you may do little more than note that what you hear or read is English.

There are, then, two aspects of the learning process, the stages of the reception system and the levels to which the material is actually analysed. The stages of the learning system will be described first, while the levels of meaning analysis will be considered in chapter three.

The learning system

While it is true that, at its best, the communication between teacher and pupil is an amazing phenomenon, there are times in practice when the child seems unable to understand what, to the teacher, is a most clear explanation of a point, much to the frustration of both! Our purpose in considering the learning system will be to see through what stages the information must pass in order to be learned, so that we may find where learning difficulties can occur and where material can be lost. A simple view of the stages of the system is given in figure 2.1. Three stages are shown, sensory memory, short-term memory and long-term memory.

Information most often comes to the learner via light or sound and is received by the senses. Sensory memory is the persistence within the senses of the information after the source has ceased. Short-term memory (STM) is where information is temporarily

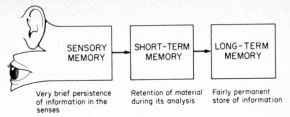

SENSORY MEMORY	SHORT-TERM MEMORY	LONG-TERM MEMORY
Very brief persistence of information in the senses	Retention of material during its analysis	Fairly permanent store of information

Figure 2.1 Stages of the learning system

held while its meaning is analysed, and long-term memory (LTM) is where the analysed information is finally stored. The most important educational implication of the stages is that while information is being received and analysed in sensory memory or STM, it is very vulnerable to loss by displacement by the input of further material. In other words, while a child is analysing the sentence he has just heard there is the danger that it may be displaced by the next sentence he hears.

The evidence for each of the stages will be reviewed.

Sensory memory

In learning, new information usually comes to the pupil in the form of light or sound waves. (The tactile reception of information by a blind learner reading braille is an exception to this general case.) These vibrations act upon the eye, or ear, of the learner. In the eye the light energy is changed first into chemical energy and this causes the nerve endings within the retina to transmit electrically to the brain. In the ear the mechanical energy of the sound vibration is transformed directly into electrical energy within the cochlea, and again there is electrical transmission to the brain.

It appears that this initial reception of information is itself, either at the receiver or initially at the brain or at both, a very, very short-term store of information. Introspectively the visual after effect of a bright light source is the simplest evidence of such a store. The rods and cones of the retina continue to transmit information of what has been seen even after the source itself has ceased to emit light. Look at something bright for a few seconds, now close your eyes and you can continue to see it, even though your eye is no longer being stimulated.

Systematic investigation of the visual, or iconic, sensory memory, stems from the work of Sperling (1960). He showed subjects an array of nine letters, such as:

$$T \quad D \quad R$$
$$S \quad P \quad N$$
$$F \quad Z \quad C$$

for a very brief exposure (e.g. 50 milliseconds) using a tachistoscope. (Basically, a tachistoscope is a box with an eyehole at one end and a display screen at the other. The screen can be illuminated for any time interval the experimenter chooses.) Sperling used two conditions: *whole report* in which subjects were required to give all the letters, and *partial report* where subjects heard a tone sound after the display which indicated which row they were to recall (high tone, top row; low tone, bottom row, etc.). He found that for the whole report condition only about four letters were recalled, but when the partial report method was used subjects could accurately recall any row. He concluded that all the information was available to the subject immediately after presentation, but that this quickly faded.

In a further study he delayed the sounding of the tone in the partial report condition and found that the percentage recall of a row which was 95 per cent with zero delay, fell to 75 per cent after 0·5 seconds delay and to 60 per cent for one second lapse. It is clear that while information is available from the senses after the stimulus source has ceased, this information is very rapidly lost.

CHILDREN'S SENSORY MEMORY

From the teacher's standpoint it is of interest to enquire how the sensory memory of children compares with that of adults. But how can we test it? The use of the Sperling task would be a bit formidable for, say, six-year-olds. The method used by Pollack,

Ptashne and Carter (1969) was to present two flashes of light one after the other. Because of sensory memory the first flash would continue to be 'seen' for a few milliseconds after it had finished and so when the flashes were very close in time they would appear as a single flash. They argued that for someone with a high visual persistence the temporal gap between the flashes would have to be longer than for someone with a low visual persistence, for the flashes to be seen as separate. They found that over the age range six to seventeen years, visual persistence *decreases* with age. They attributed this to a progressive loss in receptor sensitivity due to physiological ageing.

Does this mean that children can process information better when they are young? Gummerman and Gray (1972) found that although children have a superior sensory memory they transfer information from it to the next stage (STM) more slowly than do adults. They presented a dark screen and then showed a letter T on its side pointing either left or right for a brief exposure (determined by what gave reasonable performance with adults on a pilot study). This was followed by, either a white screen and after five seconds, a dark screen after which the subject had to report the direction of the T, or by a patterned screen (which would destroy the iconic image in sensory memory) and five seconds before report. Children did as well as adults with the white screen (which did not destroy the image) because they have a longer lasting icon, but not as well when the icon is blanked out (patterned screen) presumably because they do not transfer information to STM from iconic storage as quickly as older children. An adult level of processing was reached by eleven years.

The discovery of a visual sensory memory led to a consideration of the possibility of an auditory sensory memory, or echoic memory. Experimentation on this has been more difficult. One approach has been to try the Sperling partial-report method by making sounds come from different spatial locations and then asking subjects to report either all sounds or only those from one direction. This was used by Darwin, Turvey and Crowder (1972), who found that whole report was always lower than the partial report when the delay between sound and report signal was not more than four seconds, and that there was a decay in partial report with time.

It appears, then, that for both visual and auditory input the information remains active in the sensory memory for a few seconds after it has been received. The role of the sensory memory appears to be to hold information long enough for it to be transferred to STM. For both stores (iconic and echoic) *loss* can be caused by (1) decay with time, and (2) masking by further incoming stimuli; more images or sounds. No work has been reported on individual differences in sensory memory; could it be that a child with learning or reading difficulties is deficient in his sensory memory capacity?

Short-term memory

New information in sensory memory is transmitted to STM where it is analysed ready for storage in LTM. Evidence for the existence of STM comes from analogy with computers, physiological findings and psychological research.

THE LIMITATION ON INPUT

A basic experience in learning is that we can accept a limited input. If, for instance, you dictate a string of digits to a person and ask him to recall them (try it on someone, seven digits: 4-7-2-8-5-1-6 and again with nine digits: 9-3-7-1-8-6-5-0-4), you observe that he or she finds it difficult consistently to receive a string of more than seven. On the other hand, given a few presentations we can learn much longer strings (many telephone numbers are nine digits long). It is readily apparent that while input is limited, the total capacity of all that we can remember is very large. Now is this defect or design; disability or advantage?

Hunt (1971) has suggested that this apparent limitation is in fact an important facet of the mechanism of our intake system. Comparing man with computers, he argued that since man's environment contains a great deal of highly redundant information, the memory system would be swamped if some method of controlling and selecting the input did not exist. He pointed out that the visual system alone can provide the memory with information at the rate of over four million bits per second. He saw the peripheral memory system (STM) as the mechanism which does the selecting and ordering of important information for reception by the central memory store.

PHYSIOLOGICAL EVIDENCE

It has been observed that electrical, pharmacological and physical stimuli can act to disrupt the learning process. Electro-cortical shock, insulin therapy, blows to the head resulting in concussion and epileptic fits all lead to a loss of memory of events immediately preceding them. On the basis of clinical observations of patients having brain damage, Penfield and Milner have suggested that the initial processing of information takes place in the area of the brain called the hippocampus.

Milner (1970) described work on the effect of hippocampal lesions. A patient suffering from seizures had cuts made in his hippocampus when he was sixteen years old. After the operation he was unable to learn and store new information over a reasonably long period of time, although his immediate memory functioned satisfactorily and he could still remember events that happened before the operation. For instance, when he was tested twenty months after the operation it was found that forgetting occurred the moment his attention shifted away from the information. However, if he was not distracted he could retain material such as numbers for at least fifteen minutes by continual rehearsal. When he was distracted and then a minute later asked for the number he would not even recall being told a number. Further testing over the years since the operation in 1953 has shown that learning is still impaired to the same extent.

These findings were interpreted as indicating that information enters a short-term memory store and is then transferred to a more permanent long-term store. For Milner's patient it appears that the connection between the stores was damaged in some manner. While this interpretation supports the STM-

LTM distinction, further subjects (which are happily rare!) need to be studied.

PSYCHOLOGICAL EVIDENCE

The third, and perhaps most relevant, area of evidence for STM is psychological. Systematic study of STM dates from the late 1950s with the work of Brown, and Peterson and Peterson, which was reviewed by Neisser (1967).

Two of the major phenomena supporting the notion of STM will be considered. These are (a) the recency effect and (b) the speed of recall of previously presented items.

The recency effect is perhaps best introduced by considering a demonstration experiment (some readers may wish to try this for themselves). A group of, say, sixty subjects are randomly divided into two equally sized groups (A and B), and both groups are read a list of fifteen common nouns (e.g. house, pencil, clock, field, window, carpet, pig, flower, car, wall, table, sky, book, cup, tree). Group A are then asked to write down the words in any order they like (free recall) while group B are instructed to record the words in the order in which they heard them (fixed order recall). When the recall of the words by the

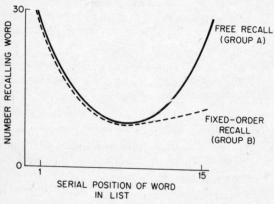

Figure 2.2 *Free and fixed-order recall for serial positions*

groups is compared they differ in the most recently heard items. A graph of a typical result is given in figure 2.2.

When you look at the shapes of the curves they are different for the words towards the end of the list. These items were the last ones heard and were likely to be still in STM when recall began. Since group A were able to recall the words in any order they were able to recall the most recently heard items first, directly from STM, followed by the items that had been processed and transferred to LTM.

Group B, on the other hand, had to recall from LTM first and while they were doing so some of the items in STM were lost. This is a variation on an experiment by Tulving and Arbuckle (1963).

The speed of recall of recently presented items has been used by Moss and Sharac (1970) to investigate the stages of processing of newly received information. In their study each subject sat at a table on which there were eight digital displays arranged in a semicircle. Each digital display had a press-button just in front of it. A digit was presented on each of the first seven displays, one at a time reading from the left. Finally, on the eighth display a digit was presented which was the same as one of those that had appeared in the series. The subject was required to press as quickly as possible the button under the display where this digit had been shown. They performed the experiment using both short (0·3 seconds) and long (2·7 seconds) time intervals between the display of each digit in the sequence. The time taken to decide where in the sequence the final digit had occurred was found to depend on the position of the digit in the sequence, as shown in table 2.1.

Table 2.1   Response times for digit positions
(adapted from Moss and Sharac 1970)

Interval between displays	Response time for digit position (secs)						
	1	2	3	4	5	6	7
Short	1·1	1·2	1·3	1·4	1·1	1·0	0·8
Long	1·1	1·2	1·3	1·4	1·5	1·3	1·0

They interpreted the results as indicating two retrieval processes, one from STM and the other from LTM. Recall from STM is faster than from LTM. Digits at the beginning of the sequence had been processed and transferred to LTM, and were retrieved by means of a scan through the sequence. On the other hand, items at the end of the presentation were still in STM when recall commenced and were retrieved directly, and quickly, from that store. For the short interval, positions one to four were in LTM, and five to seven in STM. In the case of the longer interval, the additional time allowed more to be processed into LTM, and so only items six and seven were still in STM when the presentation was completed.

The implication of these experiments is that new information is passed from sensory memory into STM where it is analysed before being transferred into LTM. This analysis takes several seconds and while it is undertaken the information is very vulnerable to loss either by the reception of further material or by the introduction into STM of distracting thoughts from LTM. It is therefore important that a child in a listening situation has sufficient time to process the speech bit by bit as it is received, otherwise the sense of some of the sentences will be lost and his understanding of the whole will be incomplete.

In considering the individual differences between learners in their ability to receive information, it should be stressed that a child who has difficulty in understanding information probably does so because his STM analysis system is inefficient and hence slow. It seems very unlikely that it is due to his STM store being physically smaller than those of his more able colleagues.

Long-term memory

Long-term memory is where material that has been analysed is stored for further use. We are not conscious of what is in LTM although we have ready access to its contents when needed. For instance, if we take something that the reader is not conscious of at the present moment, like 'rowing boat', we find it is very readily retrieved. There come into conscious thought details about boats, oars, water, river, perhaps a picture of a boat, probably some memories of rowing. Further, these memories may extend over several years and in fact to experiences with boats on quite separate occasions in different places. These have been stored together in memory and are now easily retrieved.

Several points emerge here. Firstly, LTM has, apparently, a very large capacity. We find that the more things we think about the more we find we have stored in LTM. Secondly, the retrieval or access mechanism works quite automatically and a name or description is sufficient to give recall of associated events. Further, the information in LTM is organised, for we find that details about all our boating expeditions are somehow retrieved via the general term of 'boat'. If it were not organised the recall of items would be random. A child who finds difficulty in remembering information is not likely to have this difficulty because of a small LTM capacity. Rather, the problem will be that he receives material into LTM but because of inefficient organisation is unable to retrieve it again!

Learning difficulty and the learning system

If a child is experiencing difficulty in learning the reason may lie in any of three stages of the learning system. It may be that his sensory memory is deficient and the trace of what he sees or hears fades more quickly than is average. It may be that he is slow at analysing information in STM and it is lost when he has to attend to further new material. It may be that when he transfers information into LTM it is poorly organised and he finds it difficult to retrieve later. These last two possibilities will be considered more fully in chapters three and four respectively.

While, in the long term, the teacher will want to track down exactly where a difficulty is occurring, in the immediate situation it is important for the child to have success in learning, otherwise he becomes bored and frustrated because he understands so little. Learning performance can often be improved by allowing more time for processing during reception.

We have seen that information can be lost from STM by the

displacement of further incoming information. This is demonstrated by a study by Glanzer, Gianutsos and Dubin (1969) using the free recall of a word list. University student subjects read aloud a twelve word list and then did an adding task for one, five or ten seconds. This was followed immediately by free recall of the list. It was found that the longer the adding task the poorer the recall of the most recently received words. In other words, the longer the task the more information there was lost from STM. The question now arises whether this is due to time alone or to the task. Do items fade from STM or are they displaced? This was checked in a further experiment by trying different combinations of retention interval length and task size. They found that increasing the size of the task from reading two words to six words reduced STM performance, but that increasing the time in which the task was done from two to four seconds did not. This suggests that words were lost from STM by displacement and not fading.

In more practical terms consider a child listening to a lesson, or instructions, or a story, given by the teacher. He hears a sentence and must analyse the meaning of this in STM before it is displaced by the next sentence. Now the child who is slow at processing will find that either he processes the present sentence and neglects the next, or the other way round. Either way he will not get all the information. Alternatively, he may process both only to superficial levels — but we will deal with this later. In any case loss of material will result, because it is not all being properly stored in memory.

Work on time-compressed speech supports this idea. In time-compressed speech an electronic device puts a passage that takes, say, five minutes into a four minute interval without changing the pitch. Typical results of what happens when presentation rate is increased suggest that comprehension decreases fairly linearly as presentation rate increases from normal speech (approximately 150 wpm) up to 400 wpm.

If comprehension decreases as rate increases, it is likely performance will improve if the presentation rate is slowed, particularly for less able children. Woodcock and Clark (1968) found that slowing the presentation rate down to 78 wpm improved recall compared with normal rate for children of below average I.Q. (mean 89). Normal subjects were also helped but to a lesser extent. A study by Riding and Shore (1974) attempted to facilitate the reception of a story by maladjusted educationally subnormal children (mean age 14 years, mean I.Q. 68). Performance on a recall test following normal rate presentation (150 wpm) was 28 per cent. This improved to 46 per cent at 73 wpm. It is seen that the time available for processing incoming information is an important variable affecting comprehension.

While this consideration has been confined to helping younger children who find difficulty in processing speech, the same principle also applies to older pupils who, though they can analyse language, do not find it easy to relate the new information to what they already know, and so need to be taken through the subject matter more slowly.

TO THINK ABOUT

1 Consider a child you have met who has difficulty in learning. At which stage of his learning system do you consider the cause of his difficulty is likely to be located?

Can you suggest a way of adapting the learning situation to make learning easier for this child?

2 In terms of the model of the learning system, explain why it is easier to understand a lecture when you do not make notes than when you both listen and write notes.

3

The analysis of meaning

Registering information in memory

In the early days of telegraphy a sender would decide on the message he wished to transmit, and would then tap it out in code of long and short pulses on a morse key. The code of electrical pulses would pass along a telegraph wire to the receiving station where the operator would translate the code back into the form of words used by the sender. Although we rarely stop to think about it, we use a very similar procedure when we speak to another person. We have ideas in our mind which we want to communicate. We take these and put them into a sound code which travels through the air to the ears of the person to whom they are directed. He hears the sound code and decodes it in order to register its meaning in his mind.

Information received by the senses must be made suitable for storing in memory by passing it through the stages of the learning system. This is necessary because the form in which it is retained in LTM is often different from that in which it was received. Suppose you read a chapter of a book, and on the following day you are asked to recall it. Your reproduction is very unlikely to be in the exact wording and style of the original, but you will probably express the main ideas of the chapter in your own words. This suggests that what is registered in memory is usually the essential meaning of the material rather than its verbatim form, and that the learner drops the exact visual or auditory pattern and also the precise grammatical structure and style.

The extraction of the general sense of the material is the most usual form of analysis in school learning, although other forms are also used. For instance, a literal memory of the precise form of the material is necessary when remembering a poem or the lines of a play or an important definition. Even in these cases it is the meaning and grammatical form of the information that is stored, and not the visual or auditory pattern alone. The important point to notice is that the learner rarely represents information in memory in the form that it possesses in the 'outside world', but that the information is translated into a number of memory forms.

An obvious question concerns the reason why the form in memory differs from the way in which information is re-presented in the world outside the individual. At present the answer is not completely clear because it is not known exactly how the brain stores information in physiological terms. Most probably the manner in which meaning is stored is much more condensed than the expanded form it has in speech or writing. If meanings were stored in this elaborated form they would occupy an unnecessarily large amount of space in LTM and this would be inefficient. When we speak we take the ideas we have in memory and put them into an extended structure in sentences, which we turn into a train of sound patterns. This sound pattern and its grammatical structure are probably a very 'long-hand' version of the information we can store much more briefly in the brain.

From a practical point of view, when a child listens to a teacher it is not simply a matter of his taking what he hears and transferring it through the stages of the learning system into LTM. He must transform, or translate, it into a series of forms that can economically be stored in memory. If he is to do this efficiently then he must have the necessary forms available, and undertake the translation quickly enough to allow the reception of the speech.

The memory levels
Craik and Lockhart (1972) argued that the translation of

information for storage in LTM proceeds through a series, or perhaps a hierarchy, of levels of processing. This view may be illustrated by an example. Consider the word 'blomf'. When you read it how were you able to process it into memory? Probably only in terms of either the shape of the word, or its sound. The analysis was therefore only at the *visual/auditory level*. Suppose you now read, 'It is a blomf'. You are able to take the processing to one further level, because placing the word in a sentence allows a *syntactic* analysis and tells you that 'blomf' can be a noun and is therefore the name of a person, place or thing. If, in addition, you are informed that 'A blomf is any six-faced green object', then your analysis can also include the *semantic* level, since you are able to define a blomf. When you next see a child's green cubic building block you will be able to say, 'There is a blomf'! Now the semantic level can have two forms, *verbal* and *imaginal*. You may register the concept of 'blomf' in memory either as a verbal definition, or in terms of an image or images. Finally, the extent to which new information is incorporated into your existing semantic memory will vary. Your new knowledge about blomf may be fully integrated into your memory of definitions of other solid shapes like spheres and cuboids, or it may be retained in isolation. The *accommodation* of new material is the highest level of processing. Obviously the incorporation of new matter is only possible when the learner possesses the relevant related material to accommodate it into.

It is suggested, then, that there are various levels to which newly received information may be analysed by the learner. The levels go from little more than the sensory registration of what is seen or heard, to the full understanding of the material and its accommodation into the structure of information already in LTM. Having outlined the overall picture of the levels of analysis the processes can now be considered in more detail.

EVIDENCE OF LEVELS OF ANALYSIS
A couple of studies will be reviewed which show that there are different levels to which newly received information may be processed and that the higher the level of analysis the greater the

time required for processing.

McMurray and Duffy (1972) compared the time taken by student subjects to learn twelve-letter strings of syllables which could be analysed to either the visual/auditory level or to this level and also in semantic terms. One list of syllable strings was pronounceable, and so could be processed to the auditory level, but had no meaning. The other list contained meaningful abbreviations which could be said, and these could be processed to both the auditory and semantic levels. Examples of the types of syllable strings are:

Pronounceable: BLI VEA SLE ORC
Meaningful: LTD BBC NFU RAC

They found that the mean time subjects required to learn the pronounceable strings was shorter than that to learn the meaningful ones; 3.1 and 3.8 seconds respectively. This suggests that each additional level of analysis takes time and so the higher the processing the longer the time required.

Support for this view comes from a study by Higgins (1974), who gave infant school children pairs of syllables and of words which they had to judge as the same or different. The syllables could only be judged at the auditory level. Examples were, sab-sab, bev-tev, teg-deg. The words, on the other hand, had to be processed to the semantic level, because the subjects had to judge whether the words had a related meaning, as in the case of 'finger–toes', or whether they were quite unrelated, like 'lorry–flower'. She found that, on average, the syllable pairs took 1·26 seconds to judge, while the word pairs took 1·50 seconds, or about a quarter of a second more than the syllables. The additional time was necessary for the processing to the higher semantic level. She also found that the oldest infants children were faster at both levels of analysis than the younger ones, so that it appears that processing efficiency improves as children get older.

LEVEL OF ANALYSIS AND EFFICIENCY OF RECEPTION

The higher the level to which the analysis of information can be taken, the easier it is to learn. Vincent (1974) measured the maximum number of items that could be received at a single spoken presentation, for a range of materials that could be processed to various levels. For instance, nonsense words like fep, gox, kif could only be processed at an auditory level, while a list of nouns could be processed to both the auditory and the semantic levels. A series of unrelated sentences, like 'Rubber comes from trees. Teachers work in schools', could be analysed at the syntactic level, as well as at the auditory and semantic. Processing to all five levels is possible with a series of related phrases or sentences; auditory, semantic, syntactic, semantic integration of the overall meaning and its accommodation into what is already stored in memory. In order to determine the number of items that had actually been processed into LTM, a short task was given to the children after the presentation of each word series. The purpose of this was to clear partially analysed items from STM. The task required each child to select the larger of a pair of numbers. Immediately after the task the child recalled as many words as possible from the series. The maximum size of a series that could be repeated was found by beginning with a very short series and continuing the procedure with increasingly long word strings, until the subject was unable to recall one correctly. The maximum number of words repeated at one presentation of the series by groups of seven and fourteen year old children is given in Table 3.1.

Table 3.1 **Maximum number of words repeated for various series**

Level of analysis	Mean max. no. of words recalled	
	7 years	14 years
Auditory	0·4	1·6
Aud+Semantic	2·9	4·5
Aud+Sem+Syntactic	10·4	13·6
Aud+Sem+Syntactic +Integration and Accommodation	12·0	15·6

The results indicate that when all the levels of analysis are available to the learner, reception is much better than when the material can only be analysed at a low level. Further, it is clear that the ability to process information at all levels increases with age.

LEARNING AND THE LEARNER'S KNOWLEDGE

We have seen that information is stored in memory in a form different from that in which it is transmitted. We come now to a second basic, and related, point; material is analysed in terms of what the learner already knows.

When you read 'It was a warm afternoon in late summer. The children were playing happily on the grass in the shade of the old sycamore tree' you analyse the form of each word, the syntactic structure and the meaning. How was the meaning arrived at? An active model of learning, which views learning as an interaction between the new information and the material already in memory, seems most relevant for the teacher.

The notion that new learning is interpreted in the light of previous experience was proposed by Bartlett (1932, p. 199), who cited the neurological view that the human body could only experience change in the position of a limb if the brain had some register of the position of the limb prior to the change. It was felt that new sensations from the peripheral nerves were compared with previously received sensations, and this 'standard' of previous sensations was termed a *schema.* This concept of sensory relativity was taken by Bartlett and applied to cognitive learning. He argued that new information is received and compared with what is already known. For this to be accomplished, he contended, the memory must contain prior experiences in an organised form. For him a schema referred to an active organisation of past experiences, by which new experiences are interpreted. He supported this view from his observations of the recall of stories heard by subjects, which reflected the attitudes and past experiences of the individual learner.

Piaget (1950) also drew on the ideas of biological science. He took the model of biological adaptation and applied it to human cognitive learning. Adaptation is a two-fold process of assimilation and accommodation. New material is assimilated by the learner who modifies it to fit the previously acquired knowledge stored in memory. In turn the memory store is itself modified by the accommodation of the new information. Non-biologists might find a furniture analogy useful. Imagine that you buy a grand piano; after some effort you get it through the front door, along the hall and into the lounge (assimilation). Having got it in, you realise that to accommodate it, other furniture in the room will need to be rearranged. The same sort of two stage view of reception can be applied to cognitive learning.

More recently, Ausubel (1968) has proposed a model of meaningful learning which views the new information as being learned in relation to the learner's cognitive structure. By cognitive structure he means the organised knowledge already in LTM. For new material to be meaningfully learned an individual must have available within cognitive structure relevant concepts to which new information can be linked. The lack of availability of such subsuming anchorage would necessitate rote learning of material, if it is learned at all.

The significant common point about these models is that they view learning as an interaction between the new information and the contents and organisation of LTM.

The understanding of language

So far two basic ideas have been presented. The first is that the reception of information by a learner involves its translation or analysis into forms that can be registered in memory, and the second is that this analysis is in terms of what the learner already knows. In school learning most information comes to the pupil in the form of spoken or written language. How do these principles apply to the reception of language? Let us begin to answer this question by considering the stages in the reception of verbal material. There are four basic stages, which may be illustrated by supposing that, as a teacher, you are listening to a mother who is talking about her son John who is at your school.

(1) '. . . boat.' The last word you have just heard is 'boat'. You

analyse the *meaning of the word.*

(2) '. . . his new boat.' You add the meaning of this word to others near it to form a group in order to determine the *meaning of this subunit.*

(3) 'John went to the pool yesterday, to sail his new boat'. The meaning of that subunit is now added by you to the context that preceded it. This *semantic integration* gives the overall sense of the subunits, usually in terms of the general meaning, rather than the literal form of the words.

(4) John — pool — new boat — old boat — fell in pool last week — nice boy — works hard — inventive — . . . . The new information is now *accommodated* by you into your memories of John, of his previous exploits with boats and water, his behaviour in school, and so on.

If this conversation had taken place in real life, you would have completed this analysis in a matter of seconds. Just how you would have done it is not very clear at present. Perhaps much of the difficulty of understanding the process comes from the fact that the analysis is so swift and automatic, and therefore difficult to observe. However, what is known is useful to the teacher, and can be applied practically. The stages of reception will therefore be discussed.

THE MEANING OF WORDS AND SUBUNITS

A child understands the word a teacher speaks by receiving the sound pattern and quickly and automatically scanning through memory to determine its meaning. That this process is in fact fast may be shown introspectively by considering the word 'squog'. Almost as quickly as you read it, you had completed your scan through your known words and concluded that it was not among them. The process seems to involve some sort of matching between the word read or heard and the contents of lexical memory. Sometimes when words are a fairly close approximation to what we have in memory we mismatch them, like the young London child who thought that the line of the Lord's prayer requested, 'Lead us not into Thames Station'.

In listening or reading the learner has to gain the sense of not just individual words, but of groups of words, since it is the words in combination which give sense to each phrase or linguistic subunit. For the listener the basic task is perceiving how the words should be grouped in order to comprehend the meaning. It is likely that the grouping of the words is signalled to the listener by the syntactic structure and also by pauses and tone changes.

SYNTACTIC ANALYSIS

It would be pleasant to be able to report that the part the grammatical structure plays in the reception of language is well understood. Unfortunately, despite a large number of research studies, the picture is far from clear. In view of this lack of success, the investigations will only be briefly considered, although it is worth noting that unsuccessful research can often be instructive, if one examines the reasons for its failure.

In recent years linguists have been concerned with finding linguistic models to account for the generation of language by speakers. The most well known of these generative grammars is that of Chomsky. In his early work, Chomsky (1957 — most readers will find this too technical; a simpler account will be found in Herriot, 1970) argued that there is more to sentences than a phrase structure grammar can reveal. Phrase structure grammar is the sort you may have studied at secondary school; dividing a sentence into noun phrase and verb phrase, for instance. Chomsky therefore suggested that a notion of a *deep structure* is necessary as well. This may be illustrated by considering the following sentences:

> Growling lions can be dangerous.
> Subduing lions can be dangerous.

They have the same phrase structure but an obviously different deep structure; growling is something lions do, subduing is done to them.

Put simply, Chomsky's theory was that a complex sentence is generated by the speaker by taking the simplest form of the sentence and transforming it by a series of rules. Consequently his grammar is a transformational generative one. Consider the kernel sentence:

'The girl threw the ball'	KERNEL (K)

One transformation could produce:

'The girl did not throw the ball'	NEGATIVE (N)
or 'Did the girl throw the ball?'	QUERY (Q)
or 'The ball was thrown by the girl'	PASSIVE (P)

Two transformations could give:

'Didn't the girl throw the ball?'	NQ
'The ball was not thrown by the girl'	PN
'Was the ball thrown by the girl?'	PQ

Three transformations would produce:

'Wasn't the ball thrown by the girl?'	PNQ

On the basis of this early version of Chomsky's theory, Miller (1962) proposed that people remember a non-kernal sentence, such as the passive, by first transforming it into its underlying kernel sentence and then storing the kernel along with a footnote or tag about the syntactic structure. Mehler (1963) tested this view by requiring subjects to memorise eight sentences; a kernal and seven transformations. The sentences were different in content and grammatical type and were presented in random order. After five presentations the percentage recall was in the order:

K, N, P, NQ, PN, PNQ, Q and PQ, or roughly in the order of the number of transformations.

A study by Savin and Perchonock (1965), using a rather different method, produced a similar result. They argued that the greater the number of transformations the more space a sentence would take up when processed in STM. Subjects listened to a sentence of a given transformational type followed immediately by eight random nouns and were required to recall both the sentence and the nouns. They considered that when the sentence was correctly recalled the number of nouns given would be an indication of the space that was left over in STM after the sentence had been processed. The mean number of nouns recalled for the grammatical types were:

K 5·3; Q 4·7; P 4·6; N 4·4; NQ 4·4; PQ 4·0; PNQ 3·9; PN 3·5.

At first sight such results suggest a clear relationship between deep structure complexity of sentences and their reception. However, further consideration of the methods used, and of subsequent research, casts doubt on the conclusion. To begin with, it is obvious that sentence length and sentence complexity are usually related. Inspection of the examples of sentences given above will show that sentence length tends to increase as the number of transformations increases. Since the longer the sentence, and the more complex the sentence, the greater the demands on STM, it is not clear whether the findings of Mehler, and Savin and Perchonock, are due to sentence length or to complexity, or both. In any case, replication of Mehler's study by Howe (1970) and of the Savin and Perchonock investigation by Epstein (1969) failed to support their findings. The results of these and other studies have produced conflicting results.

On the basis of more recent work by Chomsky (1965), Rohrman (1968) found differences in the recall of nominalisations (e.g. raising flowers, growling lions) of different levels of deep structure. However, Paivio (1971) argued that Rohrman did not control for the imagery of the words used. When he controlled for imagery, Paivio found no difference between the deep structure levels.

In addition to lack of control for levels of meaning, or imagery, all of the studies so far referred to have used rather artificial learning situations; (a) the literal recall of the material when in practice we usually abstract the general meaning, (b) the use of isolated sentences when most sentences we hear form part of a continuous context, and (c) the neglect of the effect of experience, since as Goldman-Eisler and Cohen (1970) pointed out, all deep structure transformations other than the simple–active–affirmative–declarative are almost non-events in everyday language.

An investigation using a passage 200 words long, as opposed to a single sentence, was undertaken by File and Jew (1973), who gave airline passengers the emergency landing instructions in different syntactic forms; active and passive, affirmative and negative. The use of the passive rather than the active did not reduce recall but fewer instructions were recalled when the negative was used.

It may well be that the present lack of success in relating grammatical structure to ease of reception has been due to an emphasis by linguists on the generation of language. It is likely that the rules for language generation are different from those for reception and that to account for reception difficulty a *receptive grammar* rather than a generative one needs to be considered. It is also important to observe that syntax is probably only a 'carrier' into which the speaker or writer puts the meaning he wishes to transmit. The listener or reader then analyses the meaning out of the 'carrier' and stores it in memory in his own form. As has already been noted, the evidence for this view is the observation that when a previously heard lecture, or a previously read chapter of a book, is recalled it is very rarely in the literal verbatim form of the original, but more usually in the person's own words and syntactic style.

SYNTAX AND THE RECEPTION OF LANGUAGE

It seems likely, then, that it is more fruitful to consider the syntactic structure of language as a system that enables the learner to divide up the language into subunits of meaning. While this view may well be an oversimplification of the role of syntax, there is evidence which suggests that it cues the division of the material into groups.

Fodor and Bever (1965) used a technique in which a subject listened to a tape-recorded sentence which had a 'click' superimposed upon it, and was required to state where in the sentence the click occurred. In recall, subjects often displaced the click slightly from its actual position. For instance, a click positioned before the word 'happy' in the following sentence was thought by subjects to have occurred after the word (the actual position of the click is indicated by 'V'):

V

'That he was happy was evident'

When other click positions were tried with different subjects, most of the errors in placing the clicks tended towards the major grammatical break in the sentence (i.e. between 'happy' and 'was'). In terms of perceiving groups of words, it may be argued that when a click occurs within a subunit of meaning, the listener displaces it either to the beginning or end of the subunit. The question then is whether it is the syntactic, or the semantic, structure of the sentence which determines the grouping of the words. A comprehensive study by Chapin, Smith and Abrahamson (1972) suggested that the displacement of the clicks is syntactically determined.

An alternative method of studying the reception of subunits is to use the findings of work on retention within STM. The work of Glanzer, Gianutsos and Dubin (1969) has shown that very recently received information that is still undergoing analysis is very vulnerable to loss through displacement from memory by the entry of further material. This displacement from STM forms the basis of the method. If the spoken presentation of prose is stopped abruptly and followed immediately by a task of sufficient size to displace the recently received, but incompletely processed, information from STM, then the recall of the last word the listener could remember hearing should be the last item of an analysed subunit. The difference between the last word presented and the last word recalled would be the subunit, or subunits, of prose that were incompletely processed. Ten and eleven year old children (Riding 1975) were told that during the reading of a story the speaker would stop suddenly and raise his hand to signal that they should write their names as quickly as possible, and that this was a test to see who was fastest. The children were not told that they would have to recall the last word they could remember hearing in the story until after the name-writing. To allow the processing to settle down to a steady state, the first 143 words of the story were read before the abrupt stop.

The results showed that, while there were differences in the last word recalled, there was a pattern of recall in that the word was almost always a lexical word (e.g. noun, verb, adverb, adjective) that preceded a grammatical word like an article or a preposition. The story was of the 'Cinderella' type in which a girl's sandal was taken by an eagle and found by a king who marries the woman it fits. The recall pattern following the stop after the word 'desert', giving the percentage of subjects recalling words in brackets, is as follows:

'. . . one of the little sandals (22)/ and was away (12)/ with it (1) over the desert (38)/'

One interpretation of these results is that subunits of meaning consist of those words between these boundaries, which are indicated in the sentences above by /.

These studies suggest that the syntactic structure of language signals to the learner the subunits of meaning into which it may conveniently be divided. However, more research is necessary to clarify this view.

PAUSES AND TONE CHANGES AS ANALYSIS CUES

While syntax is likely to be a basic means of showing the subunits of the material, there are other cues available to the listener. Two of these are the temporal pattern of the speech and the tone changes used by the speaker.

An indication of the importance of the placing of pauses in the reception of information comes from a study by Bower and Springstone (1970). They tested the effect of the temporal position of pauses on the reception of meaningful abbreviations such as FBI, PHD, TWA, IBM. Subjects listened to twelve-letter lists with helpful pauses, as above, and less helpful pauses, e.g., FB-IPH-DTW-AIB-M. Unhelpful pauses resulted in a subsequent recall that was approximately 25 per cent below that for the helpful pauses.

While work on pauses in actual speech appears to be lacking, it is likely that the learner can be helped if the teacher positions pauses carefully, particularly when the syntactic cues are not clear. For instance, at a quick first reading the sense of a sentence like, 'During that time she found it easy to fall into the habit of wondering if Albert had forsaken her and if after all her hopes were to end in failure', might not be immediately clear. Some readers will have found that they had to read the last part of the sentence twice because the syntactic cue was misleading. A comma after the second 'if' and another after 'all' would have made the reading easier and in spoken form a pause in each of these positions would facilitate reception.

Similarly, a speaker uses changes in tone to indicate to the listener how the material should be broken up into subunits. O'Connell, Turner and Onuska (1968) found that intonation affected the recall of nonsense word sequences, monotone giving poorer performance than normal voice. If the teacher is to communicate effectively with pupils, spoken language must contain clear cues to signal the subunits of the material. For this the syntactic structure should be unambiguous, the pauses should be properly positioned and of sufficient relative duration, and there should be a range of tones so that monotone is avoided.

Semantic integration and accommodation

So far, the reception process has involved the analysis of the meaning of individual words and their grouping into larger units of meaning using prosodic and syntactic cues. Once the sense of a phrase or sentence has been determined the new information it contains must be related to what is stored in LTM. When the material is a story, for instance, the newly received detail must be incorporated into the memory of the story that has already been received. On other occasions new information will not only need to be integrated into what has just preceded it, but also accommodated into other related subject matter that may have been learned some time ago.

The study of the semantic integration of newly received information into related material is still in the early stages, and has so far done little more than demonstrate that the process takes place. Dooling (1972) found that when subjects had to decide whether a sentence was *meaningful* or anomalous, the judgement time decreased as the amount of context increased. However, the time increased when subjects were asked to judge whether the sentence was *appropriate* for the preceding context.

Visual presentation was used with a temporal interval between the context and the sentence. An example and the mean judgement times are shown in Table 3.2. Dooling concluded that context affects different stages of the analysis process in opposite ways. Context speeds up semantic analysis of a sentence, but additional processing is necessary to integrate the sentence into a context.

Table 3.2 Judgement of sentence with and without context
(adapted from Dooling 1972)

Context	Sentence	Judgement time (sec) Meaningful?	Appropriate?
(none)	'The baby vomited milk'	1·14	—
'baby'	,,	0·98	0·92
'The baby was given a sour bottle before her nap'	,,	0·93	0·98

Evidence that semantic integration usually involves the *abstraction of the general meaning* comes from the style of the recalled material. Bartlett (1932) observed that, when recalling a previously read story, subjects tended to give only the main ideas and details, and their recall was very rarely verbatim. When learners read or hear several sentences each expressing part of the meaning of a complete idea, they integrate the partial information and store the whole idea in memory. The form of the overall meaning is usually an abstraction of the original. Bransford, Barclay and Franks (1972) required subjects to listen to a set of fourteen test and seven filler sentences presented in random order. Three minutes after hearing the list subjects were read a list of closely related sentences and asked to indicate which they had heard before. The test list contained potential-inference sentences whose content could be inferred from the learning material, and also non-inference sentences in which the information could not be deduced. Examples of the learning and test material are as follows, although in the actual experiment the same sentences were not used for both the potential and non-inference lists:

	POTENTIAL-INFERENCE	NON-INFERENCE
LEARNING MATERIAL	'Three turtles rested *on* a floating log and a fish swam beneath *them*'.	'Three turtles rested *beside* a floating log and a fish swam beneath *them*'.
TEST SENTENCE	'Three turtles rested *on* a floating log and a fish swam beneath *it*'.	'Three turtles rested *beside* a floating log and a fish swam beneath *it*'.

If the meaning is extracted from information and stored in memory without the literal form of the learning material then subjects should find it difficult to decide whether the potential-inference sentences were the same as the original or different. This was found to be the case; subjects could not distinguish between new and old potential-inference sentences, but they could between new and old non-inference ones. Two further similar experiments supported the view that retention is basically dependent on the general semantic content of the sentences rather than on the actual verbatim information they contain.

Accommodation of information in long-term memory

We come now to the last stage of the reception process. After the sense of new information has been determined, the material needs to be incorporated into the organised structure of knowledge already in LTM. While the ways in which memory is structured will be considered more fully in chapters 4 and 5, it may be noted here that the basic organisation appears to be in terms of the conceptual structure of the subject matter. This means that similar and related information is stored together, somewhat after the fashion of books in a library.

This process may be illustrated in school learning by considering a primary school child who has an idea of trees, and then does a topic on trees in which he learns some of the different trees — oak, beech, ash, birch, elm and so on. His new knowledge will be added to what he already knows about trees. Further learning about the different types of woods and their uses will be linked on to this. It is therefore important that each part of a subject is properly learned if it is to form the basis for future learning.

The development of processing ability

The reception of information proceeds through levels of processing. From a developmental position the application of this view will probably mean that a child needs to acquire the relevant analysis strategies for each level. It is likely that the initial levels will be learned first and this is supported by Bach and Underwood (1970), who found that, for a group of seven-year-old children, the dominant recognition memory attribute of a word was auditory, whereas for eleven-year-olds the dominance had shifted to the associative attribute. Learning difficulty at a given age could be due to a child's failure to acquire the processing strategies typical for his age.

Developmental work on the use of cues and strategies suggests that young children process information less efficiently than adults, and that they are unable to benefit from organisational cues. McCarver (1972), for instance, in a study of the recall of the position of a picture in a series, found that a combination of learning instruction and grouping cues helped the recall performance of ten-year-old and college students, but not groups of five- and seven-year-old subjects, when compared with a condition of no cues. Similar results come from Harris and Burke (1972) using serial recall of visually presented digit sequences. Grouping in threes facilitated recall for nine- and eleven-year-olds, but not for seven-year-olds. Processing ability appears to increase with age and involves the acquisition of strategies appropriate to progressively higher levels of analysis.

In terms of learning difficulty, it is probable that children whose learning performance is inferior to the typical for their age have failed adequately to acquire the appropriate processing skills.

THE IMPROVEMENT OF PROCESSING PERFORMANCE

The teacher will be interested in the possibility of improving processing ability. Kinsbourne and Cohen (1971) found that Israeli subjects performed better than English subjects of similar intelligence on consonant memory span, but no better on digit span. They attributed the superior consonant performance of the Israelis to their higher ability to process consonants, because of their experience with the Hebrew vowel-less script. This study hints at the possibility of improving processing performance by training. However, a basic problem is that most of the reception processes do not appear to be under the learner's conscious control. It is not that processing is not learned, but once it is learned it is automatically employed whenever stimuli are presented. This is nicely illustrated by Warren (1972), who showed that subjects took longer to name the colour in which letters were printed when they formed a word, than when they were all Xs. Subjects processed the word to the level of determining its meaning even though only the letter colour was required. In view of the automatic nature of the analysis processes, it is not surprising that attempts to encourage subjects consciously to employ a more efficient processing strategy have not been successful. Hockey (1973) instructed an 'active' group of adult subjects to group in threes a sequence of digits as they listened to them. A 'passive' group were told to avoid all forms of organisation. The active group's performance decreased as the input rate increased while the reverse was found for the passive group.

Conscious interference with the reception mechanisms hinders learning because it both disrupts the automatic analysis processes and requires additional processing time to employ the strategy. Two approaches to the problem of improving processing suggest themselves. The first is to use the conscious interference method over a reasonable time period in the hope that the child will learn the strategy to the extent that it becomes automatic. The second is to present a series of prose passages which are graded in terms of the complexity of the strategies they require (for instance, in the phonetic dimension, words of increasing numbers of syllables) in an attempt to encourage the utilisation of increasingly complex processing.

Practical application of the levels of processing

We have seen that the reception of material by a pupil involves its analysis and transformation through the various levels of processing. At the lower levels this involves an analysis of the sound or visual pattern of the information, followed by syntactic and semantic processing. At the higher levels of understanding, the meaning of groups of words, or subunits, must be seen in relation to the overall sense of the material, and this meaning must be accommodated into the organised system of information in memory. The analysis processes are undoubtedly complicated and, as yet, not fully understood. How can what is already known be applied to learning?

The most obvious area of usefulness is in accounting for individual differences in learning performance, and for variation within the same child on different occasions. The basic point is that the quality of learning will depend on the degree to which the learning material has been processed. Analysis which has been taken to the highest level, accommodation, will produce learning that is superior to that when processing is to a lower level. The level of analysis will be affected by the degree of attention of the learner, his processing efficiency and the content and organisation of his LTM. The effect of these three variables will be considered.

LEARNING AND THE DEGREE OF ATTENTION

Two children of similar ability attend the same lesson. Afterwards the teacher questions both about the content and finds that while one child supplies most answers, the other can find hardly any. Why does the latter pupil know so little? The probable reason is that, although he heard what was said and saw what was shown, he processed this information to a low level because he was really occupied with thoughts about another matter. The reader will probably have found that when chatting to a friend he sometimes finds, to his embarrassment, that he has not been listening, but has been thinking about other things. Or perhaps, when reading a page of a textbook and reaching the bottom of the page, he finds that he is unaware of what the page was about. When my children were young they each had a bedtime story read to them. I found on a number of occasions that while I was reading aloud my thoughts would wander to the concerns of the day, and I would not return to the content until it was time to turn over the page. Since the child listening to the story was still attentive, I realised that I must, in fact, have read it in a comprehensible fashion, although I was unaware of its content.

Schwartz, Sparkman and Deese (1970) argued that we do not remember everything we read because we do not analyse it completely. They suggested that the processing system contains a monitoring device which informs us whether or not we have the potential ability to comprehend the meaning of something we read or hear. Deese labelled this device 'the feeling of understanding'. The judgement of comprehensibility is made before, and independently of, interpretation.

In other words, a pupil can sit in a lesson and can hear what is said and recognise it to be English, but can process the information only to one of the lower levels of analysis. The effect is that after the lesson the material is not available for recall from memory, because it was never fully accommodated into other relevant and related knowledge. A pupil is most likely to use only this low level of incomplete processing when he lacks interest in the subject matter, or when he is fatigued. Students will have observed that they are most prone to this towards the end of a long lecture in a warm, stuffy room. The teacher can reduce the incidence of low level processing by making the material attractive, using variety, encouraging activity on the part of the learner, and by ensuring correct heating and ventilation.

LEARNING AND ANALYSIS EFFICIENCY

Two seven-year-old children heard a sentence and were asked to repeat it after a short interval. The sentence was, 'In summer farmers cut the long grass growing in their fields and after letting it dry, keep it and feed it to the horses in winter'. One of the children correctly gave almost all the words while the other only gave four (data from Vincent 1974). Why? Assuming that, since the material was short and this was a test, they were both fully attending, the result was likely to be due to a difference in the processing efficiency. The first child was able to analyse the information quickly enough to transfer it to LTM, while the second found that his processing system could not cope with the load and so some words were lost from STM and the whole sense could not be transferred to LTM.

The importance of efficient analysis in the reception of information was demonstrated by Miller (1956) using digit strings as the learning material. We observed in chapter 2 that the average number of digits an adult can repeat after a single presentation is seven. Miller showed that while the input limit appears to be about seven *chunks* of information at a time, by means of a grouping strategy more than one *bit* of information can be included in each chunk. He noted that digit span could be greatly increased by training subjects to group several digits in each chunk. For example, using this method many people could cope with, say, 27-43-95-62-87-34-19. Even if they could only manage four pairs they would have more digits than by the one bit per chunk method.

In order to process efficiently a pupil will need both to have the forms (e.g. phonetic, syntactic, semantic) of representing information in memory and to be provided with appropriate cues by the teacher to aid analysis. These two points may be made clearer to the reader by considering the two following examples. To understand 'Sie sind sehr gut', you will need the appropriate semantic knowledge. To readily gain the sense of 'Thel ittleb oys awt hed og', you need to know how the letters should be grouped. Just as many readers will not find the meaning of the sentences immediately apparent, so it is likely that some children find it difficult to analyse English efficiently at the auditory, syntactic and semantic levels. The basic reason is that processing is learned. Since the reception of English by an educated adult is so automatic and effortless, it is difficult for the teacher to appreciate that, in the young child, processing is much less efficient than in the adult. It is not that a child cannot process information, it is just that since he does it less efficiently, it takes longer. The improvement of reception by slowing the presentation rate was discussed in chapter 2.

From the teacher's point of view, there are two aspects of analysis efficiency; the first is being understood at the present, and the second is improving the efficiency in the future. If the teacher needs to be understood then the presentation should be deliberate with the provision of very plain processing cues, like helpful pauses, careful accenting of words and the use of simple grammatical structures. However, just as a baby will never learn to deal with solid food if he is always fed on milk, so the child will not learn new and more sophisticated ways of processing language if the presentation can always be received by using only simple analysis strategies. The teacher therefore needs to incorporate learning sessions where some complex language is deliberately introduced, so that the pupil is encouraged to develop more effective strategies.

LEARNING AND THE INFORMATION IN LONG-TERM MEMORY

If new material is interpreted in terms of what the learner already knows and has to be accommodated into the related and relevant information in memory, then how well new subject matter is learned will depend on there being in the pupil's LTM the necessary knowledge into which the new material can be incorporated. Ausubel (1968) has distinguished between meaningful and rote learning. In meaningful learning the new matter is fully incorporated into the organised structure of memory, while in rote learning the information is incompletely accommodated because the learner lacks the necessary related knowledge. Consider the statement, 'Acetaldehyde may be formed by hydrolysis of ethylidene chloride'. This may be learned at either the rote or the meaningful level. If the pupil does not have an existing knowledge of what hydrolysis is, then although he can learn the sentence by rote, parrot fashion, it is not really understood. On the other hand, if the learner already has the concept of hydrolysis and knows what ethylidene chloride is, then the new learning can be meaningful because the information can be accommodated into the structure of related knowledge in memory.

Ausubel has argued that meaningful learning is the most effective, in that it is easier to accomplish than rote, meaningful material is better retained and, since it is properly organised in memory, it can be more efficiently applied or transferred to new situations and problems. For instance, if a child understands how formaldehyde is produced by hydrolysis, he is likely to be able to extend this knowledge to predict what will be produced when a chemical related to ethylidene chloride is similarly treated.

For the teacher it is vital to aim at meaningful learning, and in order to achieve this the children must have in memory the necessary relevant information before new learning begins. For instance, if a teacher is doing a topic on Australian sheep farming with, say, ten-year-old city children, he must ensure that children are first familiar with sheep and their care, otherwise some children will lack the necessary background knowledge to give meaning to the work about Australia.

There is some similarity between building a wall and building up a structure of knowledge in a learner's memory. In a wall each course of bricks can only be laid when the preceding course is in place. In building up material into a structure in memory each new subject matter brick must only be presented to the learner when the bricks on to which it is to be placed are in position.

TO THINK ABOUT

1 A child is embarking on a new topic. Where in the analysis process is it possible for learning difficulties to occur?

2 To what extent is it possible to train a child to process information more efficiently?

3 In what ways can the teacher try to ensure that learning is meaningful?

4

Types of learning

Categories of learning

What do children learn in school, and how do they learn it? Let us go into an infants school, say. The children have just heard a story about a boy named Peter and his adventure with his dog, Rover. Because the school is on a housing estate where many children live in tall blocks of flats in which people are not allowed to keep dogs, the teacher has brought her labrador into school for the morning, so that the children can see him, stroke him and watch him having his food and water. One child, Jane, was very affectionate to the dog and even tried to hug him. Although the teacher said that it was not always good to hug dogs, she did say how nice it was that Jane was so kind to him. The children are now settling down to write a few sentences in their own words about the Rover story and will then draw a picture depicting a scene from the tale. However, in one corner of the room little Billy is still in tears. He started crying when the dog came into the room, and has not settled down yet. In fact he is really very frightened of the dog, even though it has remained quiet and placid. Most children are now writing well and some have finished their sentences and are starting on the pictures.

What will the children have learned in this lesson? Five categories of what is learned may be identified, and these are illustrated in figure 4.1.

1 The pupils will have acquired *cognitive information* about dogs, which they will have added to what they already know about them. Even though they may have seen few dogs in their

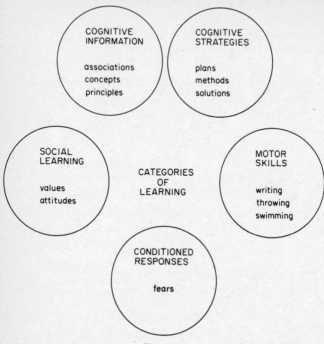

Figure 4.1

area, they will already have the idea, or *concept*, of what a dog is, and to this they will have been able to add further details, or *attributes*, about the appearance, feel, care and feeding of dogs.

2 The class will be developing *cognitive strategies*, or plans, of how to organise and use information from several sources, and to express these ideas in their own language. For instance, they will need to draw upon what they already know about dogs, upon the story about Rover, and upon their experience of the labrador, and then to put these into their own words, and also to plan and draw a picture.

3 The children will also be developing *motor skills*, such as how to control the pencil to form the words they are writing, and how to hold the crayons to colour the picture.

4 During the lesson the children will be involved in *social*

learning. As they work together they will learn to live together. They will become aware of helping, sharing and caring, as well as the less positive aspects of social behaviour. From the teacher they will learn the values current in society. For example, from the teacher's approval of Jane hugging the labrador, they learn an attitude common to most people in society, that being kind to animals is a good thing.

5 Finally, there is the case of Billy, who was very frightened of the dog. Although this fear was not learned during the lesson, it did affect the learning situation and points to the importance of teachers being aware of the nature of such classically conditioned responses.

The learning that can take place in a single lesson is very varied, and much broader than that which the teacher considers to be the main topic of the lesson.

Forms of learning

Not only are there different categories of what is learned in school, there are also different forms of learning. While the basic processing system probably works in the same way for all learning, the conditions that prevail during the learning vary. One way of viewing these forms is in terms of the interaction that takes place at the time of learning. For instance, in the learning of cognitive information, the interaction is between the new information and what is already in the cognitive organisation in memory. By contrast, in social learning, where the teacher praises and approves of the child who is affectionate to the dog, the child's emotional system is also interacting, since there is an emotional need in all people to be loved, accepted and approved of. In the case of the conditioned response, we shall see that this learning takes place when there is a state of strong physiological arousal in the learner.

Forms of learning can also be distinguished according to whether the initiative for the learning lies primarily with the source of information, or with the learner. In cognitive information learning, the initiative tends to be with the information, the pattern of which guides its incorporation into the material already in memory. On the other hand, when cognitive strategies are learned, the pupil has the initiative. He has ideas which he struggles to find a way of expressing, and when he has been successful he stores the result in memory for future use. In this respect, motor skill learning is rather similar. The child tries using his pencil to form letters, and depending on his success, or otherwise, he modifies his method until he can do the operation satisfactorily.

In general, the form of learning will be related to what is learned, and as the categories of what is learned are considered in more detail, the form of learning most usually associated with the category will also be examined.

1 Learning cognitive information

The basic processes by which cognitive information is learned were described in chapter 3. We can now consider what material is learned and how it is organised in memory.

The information in memory is linked to other items in a structure that ranges in complexity from the very simple linkage of two items, to the highly organised structure of related concepts. We may readily identify three levels of structural organisation:

(a) *Simple associations.* At the lowest level a link, or association, can be formed between just two items

(b) *Concepts and attributes.* A concept like 'dog' will be linked to the attributes such as fur, tail, bark, paws and so on

(c) *Conceptual structure.* Links can be made between a concept and those related to it. For example:

Labrador — dog — animal — living thing

All of these types of structure occur in school learning. How they are formed and the organisations produced will be considered.

SIMPLE ASSOCIATIONS
The simplest learning is a link between two items. We have

many such associations in memory. When you read, 'seven times seven', you automatically produce the response 'forty-nine', which you have linked to it. Similarly, the year 1066 evokes the name of a well-known battle, in a geographical context the name of a capital city like Paris brings the response of the country it is in, and in chemistry, symbols such as H_2O give the substance they represent.

For an association to be formed the items must be presented together, or almost together, so that they are in STM at the same time. They then enter LTM together and are stored as a linked pair. In ordinary learning situations, the strength of an association will depend on how frequently, and how recently, the items have occurred together. Hence, if it is desired that multiplication tables or vocabulary lists should be learned, they are presented with much repetition and revision.

While it is possible for associations to be stored in memory in isolation from one another, in practice the aim of most school learning is to build up a structure of knowledge within the pupil's memory which will be conceptually organised.

CONCEPTS AND ATTRIBUTES

The problem of too much information   How does your information processing system deal with figure 4.2?

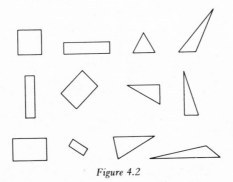

Figure 4.2

Although there are twelve quite different items, you try to reduce the information to be perceived by grouping the items according to similarities. You notice that half of the shapes have three sides, while the others have four. The next step is to label them as triangles and rectangles, respectively. This process of grouping is necessary if the memory is to cope with our environment. The point has already been made in connection with STM that man's environment contains so much information, there is the danger that the memory system will be swamped. In addition to limiting the entry of information, the problem is also overcome by reducing the amount of material that needs to be retained in memory, by grouping similar items under a common name or category to form a *class concept.*

Class concepts   We form concepts to reduce the amount of information our mind has to deal with, and this makes thinking and remembering easier. A concept exists when we make the same response to a number of similar, but often slightly different, stimuli. To all three-sided figures you make the same response of 'triangle'.

Notice that the same response is made to similar, but not necessarily identical, stimuli. Children following a nature trail through some woodland see an oak tree. A little later they see a second oak tree. No two oaks are identical, although they have very similar *attributes.* When the children saw their first oak tree their teacher pointed out the attributes of overall shape, bark pattern and colour, and leaf shape and size. This gave most of the group the concept of 'oak tree-ness', since from these attributes they were able to form a *rule.* When they came upon the second tree they were able to apply or *generalise* the rule and say, 'oak tree'. Later in the walk they were also able to apply the rule to *discriminate* between oaks and other trees like beech and elm.

Class concept attainment   The reader may obtain some idea of what a child experiences when learning a new concept by the method of receiving instances, by considering the concept of 'geb' which begins with an instance at the foot of this page and continues at the bottom of every alternate page for the remainder of the chapter.

Concepts can be learned either by giving instances of the concept, like showing a young child a circle and giving the name of the shape and following this with other examples until the child has formed his rule of the concept, or by giving a verbal definition of the rule. In practical learning situations a combination of both methods is used. This is partly because young children, in particular, find difficulty with complex verbal statements and also because the verbal definition of many concepts is not always easy. The reader may like to reflect on the definition of a common concept such as 'table' (no, it does not need to have four legs, nor even legs at all, it may hang on ropes; it does not have to be made of wood, it can vary in size over a considerable range, and you need to discriminate it from a bench, stool or shelf).

In school new concepts are usually learned by giving some sort of verbal rule together with concrete instances for the concept. For example, if you wish to teach the concept of 'llama', you could say that it is an animal that lives in South America and which is like a small humpless camel and which looks like a large, long-necked sheep. You could show a picture of the animal to give a concrete instance.

Stimulus factors affecting class concept attainment   When children learn the concept of, say, triangularity, they must know which attributes are relevant to the concept, and which are irrelevant. In this case the only relevant attribute is the number of sides the figure has. Other attributes such as size, colour and whether the point is at the top or the bottom are irrelevant, in that they do not define the concept.

Three basic factors affect the attainment of a concept. These are: (1) the number of relevant attributes, (2) the number of irrelevant attributes, and (3) the degree of similarity between

---

Here is an instance of a geb: X-X. Turn over.

the concept and others being learned or previously attained. The effect of the three variables will be briefly described.

How did you get on learning the geb concept? You found that a geb was any instance that had more than one capital letter X. The relevant attributes of geb were therefore two in number — large size of letter and more than one letter. There was also an irrelevant attribute in some instances, the hyphen, but if there were capital letters it was a geb whether there was a hyphen or not. Would the task have been more difficult if there had been more relevant attributes? We could have tested this by using other subjects with another similar task and adding an extra relevant dimension of, say, an exclamation mark. A new concept, shall we call it a 'neb', would then be capital letters plus exclamation mark.

Schvanevelat (1966) tested the effect of the number of *relevant dimensions* on the number of trials it took to learn a concept having two irrelevant dimensions. University undergraduates each learned a different concept which consisted of a line pattern. Although his concepts were in terms of the positions of lines added to a cross shape, instead of letters as in 'geb' and 'neb', the principle was the same. Each subject sat in front of a display screen, saw a pattern, and if he thought it was an instance of the concept he pressed one of two levers and if not he pressed the other. Immediately afterwards a lamp came on beside the correct lever and then the next pattern was shown. Schvanevelat used from one to four relevant attributes. The concept was judged to have been learned when the subject reached the point where he began a series of thirty-two correct consecutive responses. For a condition in which half of the patterns were instances of the concept he found that the number of presentations taken to learn the concept were 10, 40, 65, and 95 when the number of relevant dimensions were, respectively, one, two, three and four. In other words there is a linear relationship between difficulty of learning and the number of relevant attributes.

The effect of the number of *irrelevant attributes* on concept learning in children was investigated by Osler and Kofsky

(1965). They gave four, six and eight year old subjects concept learning tasks in which the number of relevant attributes was always one, but in which the irrelevant attributes varied from zero to two. The concept learning task was presented to each child on a machine. In the centre of the front panel there was a small display screen on which a shape was presented, and the child had to decide whether the shape was an instance of the concept or not (rather like the concept learning task on the lower margins of the pages of this chapter). No name was given for the concept, however, and if the child thought the shape was an instance of the concept he pressed a lever on the right of the display and if not he pressed a lever on the left. If he was correct he received a marble which could be exchanged for a prize at the end of the session.

Examples of the concepts used and of the irrelevant attributes were:

Total no. of attributes	Relevant	Irrelevant
1	Shape (e.g. circle)	—
2	Shape	Size
3	Shape	Size and colour

Examples of parts of the sequences are given verbally as follows; in the experiment they were presented spatially.

Total number of attributes		
1	2	3
circle	large circle	small blue circle
square	small square	small blue square
circle	small circle	large red circle
circle	large circle	large blue square
square	large square	small red circle
circle	small circle	small red square

The subjects were instructed that some pictures would give a marble on one side and some pictures give the marble on the

Is this a geb? x-x. Turn over for the answer.

other, and that they were to find out how to win a marble every time.

Basically, then, the task involved the child learning the 'concept' defined by the experimenter. In the examples given, the concept is the circle. No child learned more than one concept. Subjects responded until they gave ten consecutive correct-responses, after which they were deemed to have the concept. If after 150 responses they did not have the concept they were considered unsuccessful. The results of the study are given in table 4.1.

Table 4.1   Percentage of subjects learning concept

(adapted from Osler and Kofsky, 1965)

No. of irrelevant attributes	Percentage of successful subjects at age		
	4 years	6 years	8 years
0	83	97	100
1	50	60	82
2	30	40	71

As with the number of relevant attributes, learning a concept is more difficult the greater the number of irrelevant attributes.

The third factor is the *degree of similarity* between concepts. Consider three concepts learned by infant school children — triangle, rectangle and square. The relevant attributes are:

Triangle; three sides.

Rectangle; four sides, angles all right angles.

Square; four sides, angles all right angles, sides equal.

Children are likely to find it more difficult to discriminate between a rectangle and a square because they share more relevant attributes than a rectangle and a triangle do.

The degree of similarity will depend on the number of relevant attributes that are common to both concepts. For instance, a young child will find it easier to discriminate between a donkey and a sheep, than between a donkey and a horse.

Age and class concept attainment   The results of the Osler and Kofsky study show a clear relationship between age and concept learning. Ability to attain the concepts increased with age, and this was particularly so for the more complex concepts. Bourne and O'Banion (1971) investigated the effect of age on the learning of concepts having a total of four attributes. Pupils within the range of seven to nineteen years were tested on the acquisition of concepts consisting of geometrical figures. They found that the mean number of presentations taken to learn the concepts decreased from seven to eleven years, but that between eleven and nineteen there was no change in performance.

Concept learning in school   In the practical situation, concepts will be learned by children at all ages. In acquiring a concept the pupils will receive a set of attributes that will be linked to the concept name. The children in the infants class may have the concept of 'dog' as follows:

> dog — living thing
> — has fur
> — barks
> — has tail
> — has four legs
> — ranges in height from 20 cm to 1 m

Such a conceptualisation allows the child to discriminate dogs from, say, cats. However, as the child grows older he will refine this concept. 'Living thing' will probably be replaced by 'animal' and additional attributes dealing with diet and domestication will be added to allow discrimination from wolves and foxes. In general terms, then, concepts will tend to become richer as children grow older.

When concepts are taught, the teacher should try to keep the initial learning free from the presence of irrelevant attributes. For instance, when a young child is taught the basic shapes of circle, triangle, square and rectangle, the shapes should be presented in the same colour, since colour is an irrelevant attribute. If the pupil is shown each of the shapes in a different colour, as happens in some infants' class rooms, then he may

No, it isn't. What about this? XX-X. Turn over.

think that the colour is part of the concept, and that a triangle is only a triangle if it is, say, red.

While the discussion of learning has been limited to class concepts, much school learning involves the reception of *specific concepts*. The principle of adding attributes to a concept label applies to more specific concepts as well. For instance, the concept of 'Thomas Telford' deals with a particular person and is therefore not a class concept. However, the attributes of Telford may be linked to his name in the same manner:

> Thomas Telford — born in Scotland
> — civil engineer
> — worked on Somerset House
> — built many bridges
> — constructed canals

In a specific concept the attributes may also be ordered, in this case as a time sequence of the events of Telford's life.

CONCEPTUAL STRUCTURE

Links are formed in memory between concepts that are similar or related. These links may be either because the concept can be included with other concepts under a common name, for example, 'dog' and 'cat' subsumed under 'domestic animals', or it may be because a concept is dependent on others for its definition, for instance 'speed' is expressed in terms of 'distance' and 'time'. Both forms of organisation will be considered.

Hierarchical organisation of class concepts   Attempts to understand exactly how material is organised in LTM have not got very far. What is emerging is that memory is conceptually organised, and information can be stored in both verbal and imaginal forms.

Bousfield (1953) showed that a randomly presented list of nouns (e.g. bus, pea, cow, bean, lorry, carrot, sheep, car, pig) was often recalled in conceptual categories (e.g. bus, lorry, car; pea, bean, carrot; cow, sheep, pig). This suggested that information can be stored in memory according to conceptual category membership, in this case vehicles, vegetables and animals.

More recently Collins and Quillian (1969) have elaborated the conceptual organisation model. They contended that information in LTM is stored in conceptual groupings within a hierarchical structure, the position within the category being determined by the level of inclusiveness of the concept. Further, each item has those of its properties which are particular to itself stored with it and those properties which are general to the concepts in the same class or category are stored higher up the hierarchy with the superset (or more inclusive concept). An example given by Collins and Quillian was the concept of 'canary' (part of a hierarchy including 'canary' is given in figure 4.3).

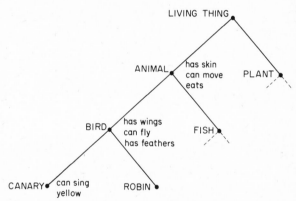

Figure 4.3 Hierarchical organisation of concepts (adapted from Collins and Quillian 1969)

The attribute of 'flight' is stored with 'bird', the superset, since most birds can fly, whereas the attribute 'yellow' is stored with 'canary' since it is particular to that bird. They considered that incoming statements are checked by a search through the hierarchical memory structure until the necessary attributes are retrieved. They tested this by asking subjects to judge

Yes, it is. Is this a geb? x-xx. See over.

statements like 'a canary is a canary', 'a canary is a bird', 'a canary is an animal' (and many similar statements about other concepts) as true or false. Statements, both true and false, were presented in random order. The time subjects took to judge the statements were recorded and the means for the true statements were as follows. Statements about category membership took longer the further the concepts were apart in the hierarchy; statements like 'a canary is a canary' took 1·00 seconds, 'a canary is a bird' 1·16 seconds, and 'a canary is an animal' 1·24 seconds. Similarly for the position of storage of attributes (i.e. a canary can sing, 1·31 seconds; a canary can fly, 1·39 seconds; a canary has skin, 1·47 seconds). It may be noted that attributes take longer to locate than category membership. These results support the view that concepts are arranged in memory in hierarchical fashion.

While it is reasonable to think that concepts are structured in memory in this way, it is by no means certain, and further research may show other organisations are in fact used. (For a discussion of the different models of memory structure and the experimental difficulties of choosing between them, see Gregg 1974, chapter 3.)

The structure of principles   A second way in which concepts are organised is in terms of their relationship to concepts which define them. Gagné (1970) has called such relational concepts, *principles*. Examples of principles are 'speed', 'volume' and 'density'. The organisation of principles is similar to that for class concepts, but instead of the concepts being included within a category, a principle is based upon other concepts which are related according to a defining rule. Consider, for example, the principle of 'speed'. Speed is the distance travelled divided by the time taken. Thus the idea of speed is built on the concepts of 'distance' and 'time' with the addition of the rule. Another instance is 'density'. The density of an object is its mass divided by its volume, and so density is dependent on 'mass' and 'volume' for its definition.

An example of the way in which a structure of principles may be built up on a few basic concepts is given in figure 4.4. In the infants school, children begin to become familiar with the fundamental ideas of length, time and mass, and by the time they are about seven years old most of them will have a fair understanding of these concepts. As they get older, on to these basic concepts they build the related principles of speed and area, and then from eleven onwards they add the principles of volume and acceleration and so on to the higher levels.

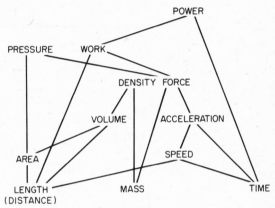

Figure 4.4 A structure of principles

From a practical point of view the important thing to notice is that principles are dependent on other concepts for their meaning and cannot effectively be learned in isolation from one another.

Conceptual structure and learning In ideal school learning, new concepts should not be taught until there are in the pupil's memory the inclusive, or subsuming, concepts to which they can be related. Very young children learn the inclusive concept 'bird' and as they grow older the names of particular birds like sparrow, starling and robin are added to it. Similarly with the concept 'tree', the category is learned first, and then the names

No. What about this? X. Turn over.

of specific types of trees are attached to it. The same pattern applies to school learning. While it would be possible for children to learn specific concepts before the inclusive ones, the presence of the inclusive concepts allows the particular ones to be related to form a structure of knowledge. The structure has the advantage that information about, say, one sort of tree is linked to that about the others and is more readily accessible than in the unlinked condition.

The aim in learning is to build up in the pupil's memory a related structure of information. Once a basic structure has been started, the new concepts can be added to it. For instance, the tree organisation can be extended upwards by incorporating other similar concepts into an even more inclusive concept of say, 'plants'. This term could include not only trees but also shrubs and flowers.

A further feature of conceptual structure is that concepts can often be included under more than one inclusive concept. For example, Thomas Telford's work could be within the category of 'canals' under the subheading of 'canal builders', as well as in the concept of 'civil engineers'. The inclusion of concepts in several categories has the advantage of providing cross-links between conceptual hierarchies.

Ausubel (1968) has stressed that for new learning to be meaningful, it must be linked to the existing structure of information in memory. This point may be made clear by considering a secondary school pupil learning the principle of pressure. In figure 4.4 it was seen that 'pressure' is fairly high up the structure of principles, and for it to be understood the pupil must have the concepts on which it is based, namely force and area. If these concepts are lacking from the child's memory structure, or are only partially understood, then the new information about pressure cannot properly be incorporated into the organisation of material in memory.

In terms of the processes of the learning system described in chapter 2, new information that is received into STM is given meaning in terms of what is already stored in LTM. The degree of accommodation that is required to incorporate the additional information into memory will depend both on its type, and the structure that already exists. If, for instance, the new material simply consists of additional attributes that can be added to concepts at present in LTM, then the accommodation is quite simple and changes the organisation of memory very little. For example, suppose a child is doing a topic on civil engineers and reads that Telford was for a time surveyor for the county of Shropshire. If he already knows several details of Telford's life, this additional one can be stored with them. On the other hand, when a pupil learns the principle of 'pressure', then the new material is an extension of his existing conceptual structure. This elaboration of the structure also incidentally provides an indirect link between the concepts on which pressure is based, 'force' and 'area'. The importance of taking into account the conceptual structure of information in a pupil's memory when planning learning will be discussed further in chapter 8.

2 Learning cognitive strategies

The second category of learning is the acquisition of strategies, or plans, of how to tackle cognitive tasks. For instance, in topic work junior school children learn how to look up and find out information for themselves. At the secondary level, pupils learn how to plan and carry out experiments in science. They also acquire the technique of planning and writing an essay. A strategy, then, is the knowledge of how to tackle a new task which is slightly different from those done before. No two topics are done in exactly the same manner, nor are any two essays identical.

A strategy is usually learned by a process of action followed by a consideration by the pupil of the result of the action. Often this consideration is guided by the teacher. For instance, when the infants' school child is learning how to express himself in written language, his future efforts will be influenced both by how his writing sounds when he reads it, and by the comments and

---

No, it isn't. What about this? XX. See over.

suggestions of the teacher as to how it could have been improved. The same processes will apply to the older student developing strategies of essay writing. The principles of critical thinking and the development of plans will be discussed more fully in chapter 6.

3 Learning motor skills

The third category of learning is the development of motor skills. Skill learning is very similar to strategy acquisition in that it frequently involves trial and error with feedback to the learner. The young child who is learning to control his pencil to form letters starts by attempting to copy a letter or word, and on the basis of what he sees he has produced, he modifies the movements he makes in order to improve the shape of the letters so that they are nearer to the pattern he is following. Since the acquisition of motor skills, once children have learned to write, is usually confined to the specialist subjects of art, music and physical education, they will not be discussed further here.

4 Social learning

In school, children learn to work together, how to share and to help one another. They acquire from each other, and from their teachers, many attitudes and values that are current in the society in which they live. Social behaviour, attitudes and values are learned in a variety of ways. For example, young children frequently learn by imitating the behaviour of others, while with older pupils at the secondary level, social attitudes are often the result of the application of logical thought. Some social learning may also be explained in terms of *operant conditioning*, and although this form of learning can be applied to other categories of learning, for convenience it will be considered here. (An extensive treatment of social learning is given in Cortis 1977.)

OPERANT CONDITIONING

An operant is an action or behaviour, and so this type of learning refers to behaviours that are conditioned. At the turn of the century, Thorndike, who was studying animal learning, found that the effect of successful behaviour is to increase the probability that it will be repeated in similar circumstances. Since the early nineteen thirties the principles of operant learning have been systematically investigated by Skinner. Operant conditioning is perhaps best introduced by describing a typical experiment.

A hungry rat was placed in a well-ventilated box containing a lever and a foodtray. (This equipment has become known as a Skinner Box.) The object was to train the rat to press the lever to obtain food. The hungry rat explored the box and eventually, by chance, pressed the lever. This released a food pellet into the tray for the rat to eat. The rat continued to explore the box and again touched the lever, and obtained more food. After this had happened a few times the rat learned the sequence. He pressed the lever, ate the food from the tray, and returned to the lever, and so on.

The rat had been trained to press the lever when it desired food. The correct response, or operant, in this case was pressing the lever, which was *reinforced*, or rewarded, by the giving of food. The motivator was the rat's hunger. It is observed that the behaviour was learned because it was successful in satisfying the need of the animal. On subsequent occasions, whenever the rat was hungry and was placed in the box, it began pressing the lever to obtain food.

While the reader will not be surprised that the rat behaved as it did, because one expects hungry rats to search for food, the principles of operant conditioning can be applied to a wide variety of learning. The basic feature of operant learning is that it can take place whenever an organism has an unfulfilled need. In the school situation such a need is likely to be emotional or social rather than physical. For instance, children have a need to be loved and approved of, and so praise and approval from the teacher, or from fellow pupils, can act as a reinforcer of behaviour.

Yes, Is this? xx-x. Turn over.

Schedules of reinforcement   Before we try to apply operant learning to the classroom, it will be helpful to consider a little more of Skinner's work. In the case of the rat, its lever pressing was reinforced by the food pellet on each occasion. Skinner found that the reinforcement of behaviour makes it more likely that the behaviour will be repeated. He also noticed that if the reinforcement is omitted, that is, in the case of the rat, if no food is given after the lever pressing, the behaviour was gradually extinguished and took place less and less often.

Skinner suggested that much real life animal learning could be accounted for in terms of operant conditioning. In the wild, reinforcement will often be haphazard, and not after every response, and so he carried out further experiments to determine the effect of intermittent reinforcement. He found that when reinforcement did not follow every response, the initial learning took longer, but that once learned, a response could be maintained by fairly infrequent reinforcement.

The shaping of behaviour   In the case of the rat learning to press the lever to obtain food, the learning appears to be all or nothing. One moment the rat is pressing the lever by accident and the next he has learned the response. However, Skinner (1953) went on to demonstrate that behaviour can be gradually changed, or *shaped*, by the careful use of reinforcement. He studied the shaping of behaviour in pigeons. In one of the experiments the aim was to teach a pigeon to walk in a right-turning circle. The experimenter waited until the pigeon was hungry and then, whenever the bird turned to the right, it was given some food. A movement to the left was not rewarded. To begin with any right movement, however slight, was reinforced, but as the behaviour was shaped, a progressively greater amount of right turning was required before food was given. This was continued until the behaviour of the pigeon had been shaped so that it would run round in right-turning circles.

In a second investigation, the object was to train a pigeon to walk with its head held as high as possible. To begin with, whenever the hungry pigeon raised its head a little it was given food. Gradually the level to which it had to lift its head to receive food was raised, so that its behaviour was shaped to walk erect.

In both of these experiments the behaviour was gradually shaped by reinforcing the required response and by ignoring the other responses.

Human operant learning Training pigeons to run round in circles is interesting if you are going to work in a circus, but the teacher will be more concerned about the application of operant conditioning to children's learning. Skinner suggested two ways in which young children's behaviour can be operantly conditioned.

Consider a young child having a temper tantrum because he wants some sweets just before lunch, and in order to quieten the child the mother gives him a sweet. The effect of this is that the sweet will act as a reinforcement to the crying behaviour, and this will increase the probability that the child will have a tantrum the next time he is refused a sweet. The mother is in fact reinforcing the very behaviour she is trying to stop. Many readers will consider this conclusion to be rather obvious. The second example is perhaps less so.

A child is sitting on the mat playing while his mother is engaged in some cooking. He wants to ask his mother a question and so, in a normal voice, he says 'Mummy'. His mother is rather engrossed in some special recipe and does not reply. He calls again, this time a little louder. His mother replies and he continues playing for a few more minutes, until another question occurs to him and again he calls his mother although this time he begins with the louder voice. His mum is by now really absorbed in her cookery and ignores the call. Seeing that he is unheeded he calls out even more loudly. This succeeds in obtaining his mother's attention and again for a while he goes on playing. Ten minutes later another question comes to him and he calls loudly to his mother. 'Oh, darling, there's no need to shout, Mummy isn't deaf', was his mother's reply.

No. Is this? X-XX. Turn over.

In this situation the mother has shaped the child's behaviour so that he shouts when he wants attention, because she only responds to progressively louder calls. While the description of this conditioning has been rather compacted and would be more likely, in practice, to happen over days or weeks rather than minutes, it illustrates the way in which a parent can, often without knowing it, modify a child's responses. In the school situation one observes that the conditioning can also work the other way round, in that the teacher is conditioned by his pupils. A teacher who has difficulty in controlling the children will often be conditioned by them to shout excessively, because they have progressively ignored his increases in volume when given instructions. He began with a reasonable voice but found that they only did what they were told when he spoke a little more loudly. On subsequent occasions this louder voice was insufficient to stir them into action, and so the volume increased slightly, until this would also not produce obedience, and so yet another increase in loudness was necessary to signal to the children that the teacher meant what he said, and so on until almost everything was at the level of shouting.

A powerful motivator in all children is the need to be noticed, loved and approved of, and this provides the basis of much social learning. In the case of the dog in the infants' class, when young Jane was affectionate to the labrador the teacher reinforced her behaviour by giving her approval, and so made it more likely in future that Jane would be kind to animals.

Approval may come not only from the teacher, but also from fellow pupils. At the secondary level, some children start smoking or experiment with drugs because they are approved of by their peers for behaving in that way. To what extent this is purely operant learning is debatable, but it is probably part of the explanation. The reader may like to consider whether the results of an experiment by Calvin (1962) can be accounted for by operant learning. He asked a group of his students to compliment all girls they met at lunch who were wearing blue. Before the complimenting started 25 per cent wore blue, but after one week of complimenting this had risen to 37 per cent.

5 Classical conditioning

The final category of learning mentioned was the learning of fears. An explanation of this learning is in terms of the classical conditioning of responses. Many children have fears and phobias that are quite irrational in that they are out of all proportion to what causes the fear. In the infants' class, little Billy was very upset by the presence of the dog even though he had never been bitten by a dog, nor was the labrador aggressive or noisy, and yet he was very unhappy. Many such responses appear to be classically conditioned. The term 'classical' is used to distinguish the learning from operant conditioning. Again, the idea of classical conditioning can best be introduced by describing some typical experiments.

THE WORK OF PAVLOV

Around 1902 Pavlov, a Russian physiologist, was studying the secretions involved in the digestive processes of dogs. One of these secretions was from the salivary glands in the mouth. Pavlov was searching for fixed physiological laws, but he found that the amount of saliva flow varied from dog to dog when a tray of food was presented. He suspected that these variations might be due to the past history of each animal and were caused by learned responses.

To investigate this he set up an experiment in which the dog stood and was held still by a harness, and a tube was attached to its mouth, so that the saliva secreted ran into a measuring cylinder. The dog was then shown a dish of food and his mouth watered, or salivated. This was a normal response. At the next feeding time, before the dog was presented with the food a bell was rung. After about thirty presentations of the bell followed by the food, the dog's mouth watered by the same amount when the bell rang as it originally watered when the food was shown alone.

In this experiment an existing response became attached to a new stimulus. Such a response is termed a *conditioned response.*

Yes. Is this? -XX. See over.

This change from an existing association to a new one having the same response may be shown diagrammatically in three stages:

(1)   Existing association

Food $\longrightarrow$ Salivation
(unconditioned stimulus)   (unconditioned response)

Initially there is an existing association between a stimulus and a response. Whenever the dog sees the food he responds by salivating.

(2)   Food (US)

Bell $----\dashrightarrow$ Salivation (UR)
(conditioned stimulus)

At the second stage the new stimulus is presented in the presence of, or just before, the unconditioned stimulus. With repetition, or sometimes after one occurrence if the situation is very dramatic, the new stimulus becomes conditioned so that it produces the original response by itself, and this is the third stage.

(3)   Bell (CS) $\longrightarrow$ Salivation
(conditioned response)

As with operant learning, the conditioned response tends to become less frequent and finally to be extinguished if the food (the reinforcement) does not follow the bell. Similarly, with intermittent reinforcement the conditioned response may be maintained. Once a new conditioned association has been formed, occasional reinforcement will keep it intact.

Having established that new stimuli could be attached to existing responses, Pavlov went on to investigate the range of responses that could be conditioned. The one we shall consider here is the learning of emotional responses.

Conditioned emotional responses   In one of Pavlov's later experiments the conditioning of emotional responses was studied by giving dogs injections of morphine. The natural effect of this drug is to produce severe nausea, profuse secretion of saliva, vomiting and then profound sleep, and so there is an automatic bond between the stimulus and the response:

Morphine (US) —————————> Nausea (UR)

The dogs were given a daily injection of morphine which resulted in nausea and other effects. After several days they began to show signs of nausea and profuse secretion of saliva as soon as the experimenter touched them, even before they were actually injected.

Morphine (US) ⟍
                                                        Nausea (UR)
Experimenter's touch (CS) — — — — — ⟋

The experimenter's touch, because it had been present at the same time as the effect of the injection, had become attached to the effect of the morphine and a new association had been conditioned:

Experimenter's touch (CS) —————>Nausea (CR)

This conditioned response is at an emotional level.

Application to human learning   Classical conditioning can be applied to human learning at the emotional level. Watson, in the 1920s, demonstrated that irrational fears may be conditioned. In the following experiment he induced fear, or phobia, for a rabbit in a young child by conditioning.

Albert, a one-year-old, was fond of a white rabbit. On the next occasion that the rabbit was shown to him a loud noise was made on a gong at the instant the rabbit appeared. This was repeated several times, after which the child was shown the rabbit without the gong. He was very frightened of it.

What had happened? The child had a natural fear of loud noises:

Loud noise (US) —————————> Fear (UR)

Yes. And this? X-. Turn over.

The incidence of the rabbit at the same time as the frightening noise gave the opportunity for the fear response to be linked to the rabbit:

Loud noise (US) ⟶

Fear (UR)

Rabbit (CS) — — — — — ⟶

The result was that the child was conditioned to fear the white rabbit it had previously liked and by which it had not been harmed. In this manner many irrational fears may be learned, even after only one presentation if the initial fear is intense.

Consider what may have happened to young Billy in the infants' class. He showed great fear of the labrador dog, even though it was friendly and placid. In his case the fear could have been conditioned when he was younger by some overly excited dog which simply barked loudly near to him. To the young child the very loud noise would produce the automatic reaction of great fear. Since he could see the dog at the same time, the image of the dog became the conditioned stimulus for the conditioned response of fear.

As another example of the learning of an irrational fear consider how a child might become frightened of spiders. One day the young child is sitting in a room with his mother when down from the ceiling on his thread comes a nice big black harmless spider. His mother lets out a scream and backs away. Because the mother is afraid, the child is frightened. This is a natural reaction. He is not afraid of the spider, but simply because of his mother's anxiety. He is then in a fearful state in the presence of the spider. The spider becomes the conditioned stimulus which on subsequent occasions brings the response of fear.

An overview of the forms of learning

Having considered the various forms of learning and their application to the school, it may be helpful to briefly examine the similarities and differences between the forms. It has already been suggested that a distinction may be made in terms of both the position of the initiative for the learning and whether the interaction between the environment and the individual is at the cognitive or the physiological level.

On this basis the forms of learning may be categorised as follows:

1 LEARNING WHERE THE INITIATIVE IS EXTERNAL

(a) *Interaction at a cognitive level.* This is the type of learning examined in chapter 3, where information is presented to the learner for analysis and storage. This may be described as reception learning

(b) *Interaction with a physiological response.* This is classical conditioning when emotional learning is involved. The learning takes place when the external stimulus enters STM when the body is in a state of arousal, and the stimulus becomes associated with that state.

2 LEARNING WHERE THE INITIATIVE IS INTERNAL

(a) *Learning dominated by the cognitive structure.* This is the strategy learning, or problem solving situation, where the conscious thinking carried out in STM directs the action to be undertaken. The result of the action is monitored by STM and if the result is successful the plan or strategy is stored; if not another action is tried

(b) *Learning dominated by the physiological state.* This is operant conditioning. The learning takes place when the individual is physiologically or emotionally in a state of need, and the action done which reduces this need is likely to be associated with that need.

The basic conclusion is that there are probably not different types of mechanisms of learning, but the form of learning that takes place depends on the position of the initiative and on the type of interaction that is present.

No. Is this? x-x. See over.

TO THINK ABOUT

1 For pupils of a given age, what do you consider to be the relative importance of the various categories of what is learned?

2 Choose a topic to be taught to a class of pupils and determine what concepts are to be learned and how they will be related to what you expect the class to know already.

3 To what extent is the structure of concepts in your memory different from that of a friend's?

4 In a primary school class the teacher finds that one not very bright child is persistently naughty. Can the teacher shape his behaviour so that it is more acceptable by using operant learning?

No, it isn't. Is this a geb? XXX. See p. 52 for answer.

5

Remembering what has been learned

The difference between the material presented and recall

'Now, John, what did we find last week?'

'Well, um, er, I don't know Sir, I can't remember.'

'Last time we thought about floating and sinking, and we discovered why wood floats while iron sinks. Can you tell the group what we found?'

'Oh yes, of course, we found that . . .'

How often the teacher is confronted with this situation! Material covered in the last week or so is apparently forgotten. This is annoying for the teacher and frustrating for the pupil, and so it is important to analyse why there is failure to recall. The difference between what was presented and recall may be due to one of three reasons.

1 The information may have been lost during reception. At any one of the stages of learning, from the initial attending to the accommodation of the new material into memory, information may not have been completely processed and so never entered into long-term memory. From the teacher's point of view it is necessary to stress the obvious point that children can only remember what they have actually learned. The teacher must be careful not to ascribe to a poor memory what is in fact a lack of initial learning. Just because the teacher tells the child about a topic and the pupil nods acknowledgement it does not mean that he has actually processed the information into LTM.

2 The information may have been learned and be in memory,

but the pupil fails to retrieve it. This problem is illustrated by the tip of the tongue experience which we have all had at some time. We find that the name of an acquaintance, or a telephone number, or the title of a book, or the name of a road, cannot be recalled although we know we know it. We would have been helped if someone had given us a cue like the first letter of the word. With more complex information a pupil's recall will also be helped by the presentation of some context. In the case of John, the teacher found that with no context, recall was poor, but that when given several cues the pupil was able to locate the necessary information in his memory. In addition to externally given cues, the way the information is structured during learning will also have an effect on retrieval. At a fairly basic level the use of a mnemonic is an instance of this. For example, the names of the Great Lakes of North America and their order can be stored by making up a sentence using the initial letters of the lakes, 'S(uperior)ome M(ichigan)en H(uron)ate E(rie)ating O(ntario)nions.'

3 A final possibility is that the information was in memory but has been lost. Whether failure to recall is due to poor retrieval or actual loss of the material from memory is not clear at present. There is some evidence that information is never completely lost from memory, but that what is missing is the knowledge of its location. Electrical stimulation of the brain with a small needle-like electrode has resulted in the vivid recall of information about apparently forgotten events. Imagine a library; if a book is accidentally put on the wrong shelf then it will not be possible to locate it using the catalogue index because it will not be in its expected place.

From the teacher's standpoint, however, inability to retrieve, and loss, have the same practical effect. In this chapter 'forgetting' will be used to denote the lack of recall of previously learned information.

The pattern of retention

Successful school learning requires that information be learned and then retained over quite long intervals. Typically, number work learned one day must be recalled again on the next day when it is used again with perhaps new rules added to it; a topic started this week must be remembered till next week when it will be taken up again; work done this term will have to be retained until next term when the class takes its certificate examination, and so on.

In practical terms the teacher must try to ensure that recall is facilitated, and this leads to the question of what variables affect retention. While our immediate response to such a question is that our memory for a piece of information decreases with time, it is important to consider the conditions that prevail when recall is attempted, the type of material learned, and what actually happens during the interval between learning and recall. Consequently the following factors must be considered:

1 The number and type of cues that are available to help the child to retrieve the information from memory.

2 The meaningfulness and internal structure of the material that was learned.

3 The amount of revision and other learning that is undertaken during the retention interval.

4 The memory style and ability of the pupil.

1 THE CUES AVAILABLE AT RECALL

In our illustration we saw how the teacher was able to prompt, or cue, John in order to help him to recall work done in a previous lesson. A typical memory experiment which demonstrates the effect of cueing (Sawyer, 1974) used eight groups of ten-year-old children. All groups listened to a short story about ancient Egypt. Immediately afterwards the first group wrote down in free recall all they could remember about the story. By contrast, the second group received a structured recall test which questioned the forty details of the story in the same order in which they were presented, so that both the sequence and part of each event was cued. The remaining six groups were given either free or structured recall ten minutes, one hour or one day after hearing the story. Both the free and structured tests were scored out of the forty details in the structured test. The results are given in table 5.1.

Table 5.1 Free and structured recall

(adapted from Sawyer 1974)

Recall test	Percentage of details recalled after retention interval			
	0	10 min	1 hour	1 day
Structured	53	45	43	40
Free	33	33	28	13

Before the effect of cueing is discussed, two obvious findings of this study may be noted. The basic conclusion is that recall decreases with time. A consideration of the possible reasons for forgetting will be considered later in the chapter. A more striking finding is that, even with the structured recall, only about half the details were remembered immediately after presentation. What happened to the rest? They were lost because they were incompletely analysed and so not stored in long-term memory. This may have happened because the listener was distracted and missed a detail, or because the detail was difficult or the story was read too quickly. Whatever the reason, the finding emphasises the need for the teacher to be vigilant about complete reception.

On the effect of cueing, or providing the pupil with information to aid retrieval from memory, the results clearly show that the structured test produced much better performance than free recall. Memory for information depends on the efficiency of the retrieval of what is stored. In this study, the cues directed the memory search made by the children by guiding them through the sequence of events of the story.

It is evident that the retrieval of information from memory is affected by the cues provided by the teacher. In practice the cues available vary from almost none, in the case of free recall, to a large number when mere recognition of an item is required. Consider, for instance, an examination question like, 'Discuss the causes of the French Revolution'. Here the pupil is given no cue except for the general area to be recalled. By contrast questions can be much more explicit, and so provide the child with aids to retrieval, as was the case in the study just described. Almost all cues will be available when a pupil answers a multiple-choice test, where he only has to recognise the correct response. There are, then, three general degrees of cueing, which in ascending order are: free recall, structured recall and recognition.

What is measured by a recall test will depend on the type of test. For instance, a multiple-choice test will assess whether information is in memory but not how good the pupil is at finding it. In everyday life it is probably true that all levels of recall are needed. An assistant in an ironmonger's shop will need to be able to recognise whether bossing mallets are stocked. At the level of recall, a TV repairer faced with a television set that fails to produce a proper picture must be able to retrieve the possible reasons for the fault, so that he can work out a test procedure. Since retrieval ability is important pupils should be encouraged to practise it. Children who are poor at remembering may have the difficulty because they do not efficiently catalogue and organise new information so that it can be readily retrieved later. More research is needed to determine how material is located in, and retrieved from, memory.

2 THE ORGANISATION OF INFORMATION IN MEMORY

In addition to external cueing, the recall of information is also affected by the way in which it is organised in memory. There are two aspects of its organisation: (a) the way in which it is related to other similar information in memory, and (b) the internal structure of the material itself.

The relationships in memory In chapter 3 a distinction was made between meaningful learning in which new material is accommodated into the structure of information already in memory, and rote learning where it is not. These degrees of relationship represent the extremes, and in practice it would be unusual for learning to be completely rote or completely meaningful. In most material even the least able children will be able to find a link between some of the details and what they already know, while the brightest will find some terms unfamiliar to them.

While a teacher would not deliberately present material that could not be made sense of by the pupils, it does sometimes happen that information is meaningless for a child because he has not the necessary knowledge to relate it to. The material is then rotely learned as an isolated chunk which is not related to the other knowledge in memory. It is therefore instructive to look at the fate of rotely learned information. In a classical study Herman Ebbinghaus, in the six years preceding 1885, investigated the recall of nonsense material. He used himself as the subject and he learned lists of thirteen nonsense syllables, e.g., HIJ, XOT, KEV, RUL, SIH, etc. He then measured how well he remembered these lists after intervals of time varying from twenty minutes to one month after learning. He learned each list until he could repeat it correctly twice without hesitation, and he noted the time taken to learn it. He tested his retention by observing the time it took him to relearn the list, and the percentage saving in time (e.g. 1,000 seconds to learn, 600 seconds to relearn, saving 400 seconds, or 40 per cent of the original time). With great diligence Ebbinghaus learned and relearned 1,200 lists. The results are shown in table 5.2.

Table 5.2   The retention of nonsense syllables

Time since learning	20 min	1 hr	1 day	2 days	6 days	31 days
Mean percentage saving	58	44	34	28	25	21

He found that within one hour he had forgotten more than half of what he had learned, and this loss increased in two days to nearly three-quarters of the material. Such a rate of forgetting would be very disheartening for both teacher and learner, but then this was rote learning in which the material was not readily relateable to other information already in memory and so was not easy to retrieve. It was also verbatim learning in which the exact words had to be retained rather than, as is the case for most school learning, the general meaning.

Children who appear to forget newly learned information very quickly are likely to be learning by rote. The material was probably not very meaningful to them and so they learned it without relating it to the rest of memory. This type of learning is discouraging for the pupil, and can be guarded against by testing for understanding during learning.

The structure of the learning material   The structure of what is learned will also provide the pupil with a means of organising it in memory which will affect its retrieval. To illustrate this the retention of a story and of a descriptive thematic passage will be compared. Story material has an inbuilt serial structure because the details of the narrative follow a sequence. By contrast, thematic passages containing lists of facts could be presented in almost any order and lack an underlying sequential organisation. For instance, a passage describing life in an Indian village could deal with the topics of family size, styles of dress, cooking methods, religious beliefs, housing and so on in any order. Sawyer (1974) compared the retention of a short story with that of a thematic passage describing the natural history of emperor penguins. Both passages were 190 words long and were of similar difficulty in terms of the numbers of difficult words and sentence length. Ten-year-old children were randomly assigned to four groups. The first group listened to the story followed by immediate free recall in which subjects wrote down all they could remember. The second group heard the story and recalled it after twenty-four hours. Groups three and four received the penguin passage and recalled it immediately, and after twenty-four hours, respectively. The recall was scored by dividing the passages up into details; fifty-eight in the story and sixty in the penguin passage. The percentage of details recalled is given in table 5.3.

Table 5.3　Free recall of story and thematic passage

Passage	Percentage of details recalled	
	Immediate	After 24 hours
Story	39	19
Thematic	37	26

It was found that although there was little difference between the immediate recall scores, the penguin passage was better recalled after twenty-four hours. Serially structured information was less well retained than conceptually structured material.

3 AMOUNT OF REVISION SINCE LEARNING

Since information is forgotten over time, the teacher is faced with the practical problem of how to maintain material in the pupil's memory during the period between its first being learned, and such time as it should be recalled for relation with new learning or for a terminal test. Retention is maintained by means of revision.

Let us suppose that the material a teacher presents will be recalled for, say, an examination in ten weeks time. What form should the revision take and at what points during the retention interval should it be given? There are two forms of revision, retest and review, and these have different functions. Retest is requiring the pupil to recall the subject matter in order to maintain its availability in memory. Review involves presenting the subject matter, or a condensed version of it, in order to replace in memory any details that have been forgotten. Obviously a retest will only maintain in memory what is still there and is of little use when much forgetting has taken place, but there is evidence that it is better than review at maintaining material in memory. The choice of revision method will therefore depend on how much forgetting has taken place.

Consider figure 5.1(a) which shows a typical retention graph. Information is forgotten more quickly to begin with and more slowly later on. Suppose the teacher has a revision session after two weeks by giving a retest of what was learned (see figure

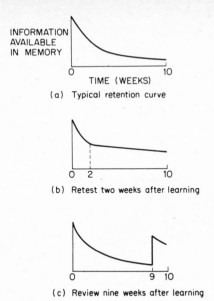

(a) Typical retention curve

(b) Retest two weeks after learning

(c) Review nine weeks after learning

Figure 5.1 The effect of revision on retention

5.1(b)), this will maintain the availability of the material in memory and improve performance in the examination at ten weeks. Alternatively, the teacher may give a review, as in figure 5.1(c), one week before the examination and this will put back into memory much that has been forgotten.

Sones and Stroud (1940) looked at the relative effects of testing and review at various temporal positions during retention. Groups of twelve-year-old pupils were given twenty minutes to read a 1,750 word article on the history of paper and methods of paper making. The groups were then given revision by either testing or rereading at a point during the seven week retention period, after which a forty-item multiple choice test was given. The groups received the revision on either first and third days, or eighth and fifteenth days, or fifteenth and seventeenth days. The revision test was a thirty-item multiple choice test. The mean recall scores (out of forty) on the final test are given in table 5.4.

Table 5.4   Mean score on test after seven weeks

(adapted from Sones and Stroud 1940)

Type of revision	Position of review after learning (days)		
	1 and 3	8 and 15	15 and 17
Test	17·8	15·7	15·2
Rereading	16·0	16·4	16·9

It is clear that in their experiment the most effective revision was the test at first and third days. However, as has been suggested, testing became progressively less useful as the time since learning increased. By contrast, the effectiveness of rereading increased with time. While the exact placement of revision will depend on the particular material and the length of the retention interval, this experiment does guide the teacher in choosing and placing an appropriate revision activity.

Retention and further learning   We come now to a second aspect of revision. In practice, except in connection with terminal examinations, revision is rarely an activity that occurs in isolation from further learning. Typically, material that was learned on a previous occasion is reconsidered and to it is added further new information. In other words, learning is cumulative. An infants' school child learns about addition and then later, into this knowledge, incorporates the idea of multiplication. An older child may do a topic on Tudor England and then later some work on the Jacobean period, and this must be related to, and will involve, the recall of some of the previously learned material. At the secondary level a pupil learning about the physical concept of pressure will have to recall the concepts of force and area upon which the definition of this one depends.

Since new meaningful learning of necessity requires the recall of related information, a form of revision happens incidentally whenever further material is learned. The positioning of further learning, relative to the previous learning on which it depends, should be such that forgetting will not be too great otherwise formal revision will need to be incorporated. The sequencing of learning material will be considered in chapter 8.

Not only will the temporal position of the new information be important, but also the way in which the new material relates to the existing will affect the retention of what had been learned previously. When the form and content of the new material is very *similar* to the existing material, the recall of the first learned material may be lessened. Kalbaugh and Walls (1973) gave groups of thirteen-year-old children several 210-word science passages about minerals which were very similar in content and format. Each dealt with a different mineral, e.g. quartz, calcite. Recall of the first passage immediately and after two days was compared with the number of passages interpolated between it and final recall. The recall performance on the randomly ordered item completion test is given in table 5.5.

It is clear that learning similar, related material has a retroactive effect, and can make the recall of the initial learning difficult. It must be noted that this degree of similarity probably only occurs in the lists of properties of materials, and even there a teacher can do much to structure the material so that repetitive similarity is avoided.

Table 5.5   Recall of the first passage presented

(adapted from Kalbaugh and Walls 1973)

No of interpolated passages	0	2	4
Recall after 2 days as percentage of immediate	91	78	72

Another aspect of the learning of similar materials was studied by Kalbaugh and Walls which compensates for the loss of the initial passage. They found that when similar passages are learned *prior to* the test passage, the greater the number of passages the better the immediate recall of the test passage. This was attributed to a learning to learn effect.

When interpolated material is related, but dissimilar in structure, the effect on recall tends to be helpful. Ausubel, Stager and Gaite (1968) found that when learning is followed by interpolated material that is related in substance, so that cumulative learning typical of school can take place, then recall of the first passage is facilitated rather than hindered. In order to simulate a real learning situation, they had three learning materials, each approximately 2,000 words long — one on Zen Buddhism, another on Buddhism and a third on drug addiction. The first and second passages obviously contained related information, while the third did not. One group of student subjects read the Zen Buddhism passage for forty minutes and then two days later the drug addiction piece, followed after two days by the information about Buddhism, and then after three more days a recall test of the first passage about Zen Buddhism. A control group followed the same pattern except that they received the drug addiction material for a second time in place of the Buddhism passage. Although the Buddhism passage did not provide any answers for the recall test, the experimental group had a higher recall score than the control (respectively 11·4 and 9·9 out of a maximum of 31).

It would appear that in usual school learning, the reception of information related to previous learning improves the availability of the subject matter in memory. This will be due in part to the revision effect, and also perhaps to an improvement in the organisation of the material in memory as it is built up into a more complete structure.

4 MEMORY ABILITY

Shuell and Keppel (1970) have argued that apparent variation in memory performance between individuals is attributable to differences in how completely the information is learned rather than differences in memory ability. They divided a group of ten-year-old children into slow and fast learners on the basis of the number of words they recalled after one presentation of a list of nouns. A previous study had shown that when fast learners were presented with the words at a rate of one per second they learned the same number from the list on average as when slow learners received the words at one per five seconds. The fast and slow learners received a list of nouns at these respective rates.

Half of each group recalled the list immediately and the rest after two days. The mean numbers of words recalled by the fast and slow groups were, respectively, 8·2 and 8·7 immediately, and 3·6 and 4·1 after two days. These results suggest that differences in recall are in fact due to variations in learning performance and not memory ability.

While it is certainly true that apparent differences are often due to learning difficulties, Conry (1976) failed to support Shuell and Keppel's findings when a prose passage was used as the learning material. Ten-year-old pupils from a wide ability range listened to the passage and were given a structured recall test. This was repeated for each subject until perfect recall was achieved. One week later the subjects were again given the recall test. Recall score was found to decrease linearly as the number of presentations necessary for the initial learning increased. The mean recall score varied from a maximum of sixteen where learning took only one presentation to one when seven presentations were required. (The correlation between the number of presentations to learn and recall after one week was −0·86.)

It appears that in a typical school, children do differ in their ability to remember. While this area needs to be further researched, some pupils are probably able to organise the material more effectively in memory than others, and this makes subsequent recall more efficient.

Theories of forgetting

An obvious question is, 'Why do we forget at all?' The teacher would find it so convenient if children could readily recall everything they had learned whenever they needed to. Students faced with the prospect of examinations are likely to feel this even more strongly! We know that we do forget, but at present research into memory and the mechanisms of the brain has not proceeded far enough to tell us exactly why. Some idea of the problem of finding out how the brain works may perhaps be gained by imagining a large school hall crammed from floor to ceiling with transistor circuits like those in a radio or television set, and then the whole lot compressed into a box the size of the brain. The circuits in the brain are so tiny and complex, and there are so many of them, that the exact working has not been determined. There have been three general theories of forgetting.

1 *The trace decay theory*   This is the idea that what is learned makes some sort of trace or change in the brain cells. This trace then gradually fades away with time, perhaps in the way that marks in the sand slowly weather away. This is an old idea and it has an intuitive attractiveness. It is simple and fits in with a possibly parallel phenomenon, the visual after-effect. When you look at a bright light and turn your eyes away, there remains in your vision an image of the light. This is because the light affected the cells in your eye and caused a chemical change in them. Fairly quickly the chemical returns to its original state and the after-image disappears. If it happens in the eye, perhaps the brain has similar chemical cells and memory is recorded by electro-chemical changes. The fact that the theory is plausible is, however, insufficient if it cannot be demonstrated. At present the study of the physiology of the brain has not reached the stage of understanding exactly how information is stored.

2 *The interference theory*   Consider the following study by Jenkins and Dallenbach (1924), who investigated the difference between retention while awake and retention while asleep. Two student subjects learned a serial list of ten nonsense syllables until they could correctly repeat the list. One subject learned the list early in the morning and then had to recall it later in the day. The other learned the list immediately before going to sleep at night and then recalled the list on waking. This was repeated for retention intervals of 1, 2, 4 and 8 hours, with a different list for each interval, and both subjects tried them for waking and sleeping. The results were striking and almost identical for both subjects, and are given in table 5.6. Notice that after eight hours the difference between the sleeping and the awake retention

suggests that during sleeping much less is forgotten. Why? Jenkins and Dallenbach suggested that forgetting is not so much a matter of the decay of old impressions and associations, as it is a matter of *interference*, or the inhibition of the old by the new.

Table 5.6   Recall after sleeping and waking intervals
(adapted from Jenkins and Dallenbach 1924)

Interval activity	Recall at intervals since learning (hrs)				
	0	1	2	4	8
Asleep	10	7	5	6	6
Awake	10	5	3	2	1

McGeoch and McDonald (1931) investigated the interference effects of different degrees of similarity of new to earlier learning. They used the pattern, learn A, learn B and recall A. With university student subjects they found that the learning of new material after the perfect learning of A caused the subsequent recall of A to be less. The A material was to learn a list of adjectives to perfection and following this different groups had different B learning tasks before the final recall of A. The interpolated, or B, activities, together with the percentage of adjectives recalled, are given in table 5.7.

Table 5.7   Recall after interpolated learning
(adapted from McGeoch and McDonald 1931)

Interpolated activity	Percentage of adjectives recalled
Rest (reading jokes)	45
Learning nonsense sylls	26
Learning unrelated adjs	22
Learning synonymous adjs	12

The more similar the new learning to the old, the greater the degree of interference.

These studies used nonsense syllables and word lists as learning material and the conditions were very different from those in normal meaningful learning in the school. Newman (1939) repeated the Jenkins and Dallenbach experiment using meaningful stories instead of nonsense syllables. He asked eleven college students to read three short stories, each about 300 words long. They read each story at a different time of day (morning, afternoon and night) and recalled it after approximately eight hours. The order of the stories was rotated into roughly equal numbers of each type during the morning, afternoon and evening. Unknown to the subjects, Newman had divided the material of each story into essential and non-essential details. The essential details were the main points of the story, while the non-essential were incidental details. He found that for the non-essential details the amount recalled after sleeping was 47 per cent, compared with 25 per cent after morning learning and 19 per cent after afternoon learning. This was in agreement with Jenkins and Dallenbach. However, he found no real difference between the retention of essential details, 87 per cent after sleep, 84 per cent after morning learning, and 87 per cent after afternoon learning. Newman concluded that the organised character of meaningful learning significantly reduces the effect of interference.

3 *The assimilation theory*   In view of the lack of interference in the retention of meaningful material typical of school learning, Ausubel (1968) proposed a theory to account for the forgetting of material that was understood when learned, which he termed the assimilation theory.

Let us suppose that you have the class concept of 'tree', which is a fairly inclusive concept. Suppose further that you read a book on tree identification which tells you about the different types of trees, oak, beech, elm, ash, birch, etc. You now have the inclusive concept of tree with the more specific concepts of oak and beech added to it. Let us further imagine that a long time now elapses when you make little use of your knowledge. The memory is an active thing and as new learning takes place it does some clearing up to make room for the new material. It does this by grouping together concepts which are similar and which do not seem to have been used for some time. During this clearing up it comes across tree, oak tree, beech tree, and so on, notices that they are not used much and tidies up by putting them all together as meaning the same thing, that is 'tree'. When you later look at trees with a view to identification all you can recall is 'tree', and no longer the various types.

This, very roughly, is Ausubel's theory. Learning is an extension of more inclusive concepts, and so he argued that forgetting is the reverse, the assimilation of information that is not used back into more inclusive related concepts.

In the long term it will probably emerge that each theory is part of the truth, and that the whole picture is rather complex.

The forms in which information is stored

The abstraction of meaning   Bartlett (1932) noticed that when subjects recalled a story they had read, they rarely gave a verbatim account, but rather expressed the main sequence of events in their own words. This, and the other work on semantic integration discussed in chapter 3, suggests that information in memory is in terms of the sense of the material and not usually in an identical form of words. When pupils read or hear something they abstract out of it the essential meaning and store that. Later, at recall, they express this idea in their own words.

Verbal and imaginal aspects of semantic memory   It appears that information can be stored in more than one form. Consider the sentence, 'The two boys stood on the old stone bridge and looked at the glistening water of the stream as it hurried over the stones.' As you read that sentence and analysed its meaning your processing system could have represented the sense in either verbal or in imaginal form, or in both. The verbal form is in terms of word meanings, while the imaginal is a visual representation of the scene.

Paivio (1975) has argued for such a dual representation theory of memory by drawing support from physiological and psychological studies. The brain contains two halves, or hemispheres, one on the right and the other on the left. The left hemisphere controls the right part of the body and the right hemisphere the left. In most people the left hemisphere is dominant, as is shown by their being right handed. Verbal memory seems to be located in the dominant hemisphere, while the imaginal memory is in the other. So for most people the left hemisphere deals with verbal memory, while the right contains the imaginal memory. Damage to the right side of the brain impairs visual memory, but does not affect verbal memory, and vice versa. Further support for the dual view of LTM comes from the finding that verbal memory is interfered with more by listening then by seeing new information. Paivio contended that the two forms are to some extent independent of one another. In chapter 7 individual differences in preference for either the verbal or imaginal form of representation will be considered in relation to learning performance.

Memory structure An important aspect of memory is its organisation. As an illustration, suppose that a child hears the following lists of words and is asked to recall each list in any order.

(a) Red, orange, yellow, green, blue, indigo, violet

(b) Bus, dog, cat, lorry, rabbit, car, van.

There are at least three ways in which he may structure the information in memory: (1) according to the presentation order of the words, (2) in terms of their sequential structure, and (3) on the basis of the conceptual similarity of the items.

These ways of organising information may be applied to most school learning, but word lists were chosen because the structures are easy to illustrate. The first list can be stored according to its presentation order, and also in terms of its serial structure, since the colours are in the order of those in the rainbow. These two ways support one another. Because all the words are colours no conceptual grouping other than into a single category is possible. By contrast, the second list may be stored according to its presentation order, but it possesses no particular sequential structure. It can, however, be organised in terms of the conceptual groupings of 'vehicles' and 'animals' (i.e. bus, lorry, car, van; dog, cat, rabbit), as in the Bousfield work mentioned in chapter 4 (p. 56).

The most enduring form of organisation is probably the conceptual grouping, followed by serial structure, and then presentation order. This is supported by the findings of the study already described in which the thematic passage about the penguins was better retained than the story which had a serial structure.

Some conclusions about retention

The importance of memory in education is rather under-estimated at the present time. While the rote cramming of facts is to be avoided, successful cumulative meaningful learning relies very heavily on an efficient memory. Although the reasons for forgetting are not yet understood, research findings indicate that children can retain information over a long time period if certain basic conditions are fulfilled.

1 The material must actually be learned to begin with, since only what has been learned can be retained.

2 The teacher can help recall by providing cues to enable the pupil to retrieve information from memory.

3 The learning should be meaningful and the material structured so that it is self-cueing.

4 The teacher must ensure that there is adequate revision if the retention period is long, and can aid memory by planning the learning programme so that there is frequent incidental recall.

5 Children who are poor at retaining information will need more frequent revision than others, and so individual differences in retention ability should be catered for.

TO THINK ABOUT

1 What levels of retention (e.g. recognition, recall), over what time intervals, are typically required in school?

2 Is all school learning cumulative learning?

3 What retrieval cues are usually given in school? Does the provision of a large number of cues (as in Nuffield Science multiple-choice examination papers) result in a different type of learning from that where few cues are given?

4 For a pupil who has difficulty in retrieving information he has learned, design a programme of activities to improve his retrieval performance.

6

Learning and guidance

The choice of learning method

In school learning the teacher is faced with a choice; should the pupils discover new information and concepts for themselves, or should this knowledge be presented to them in a form that is ready to assimilate? For instance, in the infants' school the basic shapes such as a square, circle and triangle can be learned either by the teacher showing the shapes and describing the attributes of each, or by showing a shape and asking what it is, telling the child whether he is right, and then showing further instances until the child has the concept. With older children, should the teacher present the principles of balance by giving the principles and demonstrating them, or should he give the pupils a metre stick, a wedge to balance it on, and some weights to hang from it, and ask the children to discover the rules for making the weights on one side balance those on the other?

Before discussing this choice in detail it is necessary to consider the processes of problem solving and critical thinking that are essential to discovery. The basic question is under what conditions and with what prior knowledge can a child best make discoveries? The problem in trying to answer this question, as in other areas, is that little research has been done with children.

Critical thinking and problem solving

Every day we meet situations which are to some degree new to us and which require us to use our knowledge in a way that is different from the ways in which we have used it in the past. Many of these problem situations involve so little critical thinking that we hardly recognise them as problems to be solved. For example, adding up a list of numbers we have not previously summed, or opening a door in a building that is new to us, or writing a letter. Other situations are very obviously problem ones, such as working out why the car has broken down, starting on an essay, or finding out why the lights have fused.

THE BASIC PATTERN OF PROBLEM SOLVING

It is possible to distinguish between *productive* thinking, in which a novel way (for the individual, at least) is found to solve a problem, and *reproductive* thinking, where a previously worked

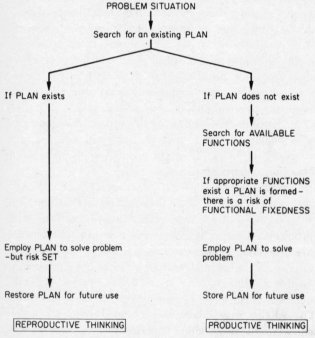

Figure 6.1 Productive and reproductive thinking

out plan is employed. Consider a young child doing some productive thinking about a problem situation. While his mother's back is turned there is the opportunity to raid the biscuit tin, but it is on a high shelf well out of reach. What is he to do? Following figure 6.1, he searches for an existing plan but finds none, so he must form one. He considers the available functions of objects in LTM. What about a kitchen stool for climbing on to make himself taller? He stands on one but still cannot reach. He searches memory for other objects that have the function of reaching things. A stick, he thinks. He fetches a stick, climbs on the stool and is just dislodging the biscuit tin from its shelf when his mother returns to the kitchen. Never mind, he can now store the plan for future use!

In terms of the basic model of learning described in chapter 2, problem solving is monitored by STM acting in an executive capacity. Information about the problem is assessed by STM, which then initiates searches of LTM for an appropriate plan. If a suitable plan is not found, STM investigates the possibility of producing a solution by utilising and combining in a new way what is already known. After each attempt at solving the problem, STM evaluates the result. If it is unsatisfactory, other combinations of ideas are tried, until either a solution is found or STM deems the problem insoluble.

The formation of plans

THE SEARCH FOR AVAILABLE FUNCTIONS

In considering the formation of plans for solving problems, early workers in this field noted that new problems are solved by the right combination of past experiences. Duncker (1945) introduced the idea of *available functions*. This notion was clarified by a study by Saugstaad and Raaheim (1960), who investigated the effect of past experience on problem solving. The subjects were seventeen-year-old secondary school pupils who were studying science. An experimental group were given a bent nail and a tube made from a sheet of paper and asked to state as many functions or uses for them as they could. A control group were not given the objects. All subjects were then individually tested on the problem, which was as follows. The subject stood behind a chalk line, 260 cm in front of which was a glass jar containing some small steel balls and standing in a movable wooden frame. Beside it was a metal container. The task was to transfer the steel balls from the glass container to the metal one without crossing the line. The subject was given four newspapers, a long piece of string, a pair of pliers, five elastic bands and an iron nail. The solution was to bend the nail into a hook with the pliers, attach the string, cast the hook and pull in the frame with the glass jar in it, make a paper tube out of the newspapers and elastic bands and send the balls down the long tube into the metal container. The performance of the subjects is shown in table 6.1.

Table 6.1 **Performance on transfer problem**

(adapted from Saugstaad and Raaheim 1960)

Group	Percentage successful	
	After 15 minutes	After 25 minutes
Experimental	85	95
Control	7	20

It is clear that having the relevant functions of objects readily available in LTM is critical for success in solving a novel problem. The control group who had not thought about the functions of the objects available to solve the problem were both slower and less successful than the experimental group.

Applying this finding to the school, it may be noted that pupils cannot be creative out of nothing, but rather that creativeness is the ability to combine previous experiences in a new way. The implication is that children must have a wide variety of experiences and knowledge to draw on if they are to be creative. Further, problem solving without hints and direction can be very time consuming.

THE RESTRICTION OF FUNCTIONAL FIXEDNESS

Duncker noted that the previous use of an object made it less readily available in a future problem solving situation where it was necessary to use the object in a different way. This prompted an experiment by Birch and Rabinowitz (1951). The subjects were engineering students. An experimental group R received training in the completion of an electrical circuit by the use of a relay. A second experimental group S was trained to complete the circuit using a switch. A control group was given no training. Both the switch and the relay were compact, fairly heavy items, that could easily be tied to the end of a cord.

Shortly after having completed the pre-training tasks the subjects were individually presented with the problem. Each subject was taken into a room which was bare of all furniture. From the ceiling hung two cords which were too far apart to permit one to be held and brought to the hanging end of the other. The problem was to tie the hanging ends of these cords together using as an aid only the objects provided, which were a switch and a relay. The solution was to tie either object to the end of one cord, set it swinging like a pendulum and then draw the other cord towards it and catch the object when the cord swung within reach. The aim of the experiment was to see to what extent the pre-training experience of the switch and the relay affected the choice of object to act as the pendulum bob in solving the problem. The frequency of choice of the objects is given in table 6.2.

Table 6.2   Choice of object for pendulum weight

(adapted from Birch and Rabinowitz 1951)

Group	Percentage choosing as weight	
	Relay	Switch
Control	50	50
Experimental R (relay)	0	100
Experimental S (switch)	78	22

The subjects who received no training (control) did not show preference for either the relay or the switch; half chose one while the rest used the other. The experimental group R, having used the relay in the electrical training, all used the switch in the pendulum task, while group S also showed preference for the item they had not used. It is seen that subjects were hindered in using an object for a function other than the one to which they were accustomed, when faced with a new problem. Objects that had been seen as electrical could not be viewed in terms of their general characteristic of mass which was necessary for the pendulum construction. The search for available functions is limited by functional fixedness.

PLANS ARE STORED FOR FUTURE USE

When a problem is successfully solved for the first time, a plan has been devised for its solution. Miller, Galanter and Pribram (1960) defined a plan as a process that can control the order in which a sequence of operations is to be performed. A plan, for us, is very similar to a programme for a computer. The notion of a plan bears some similarity to Piaget's concept of 'schema'. Once we have solved a problem we store the plan so that on future occasions we can quickly solve similar problems by applying the plan; this saves having to solve the problem from scratch. Some examples of plans originally learned and stored are how to tie a knot, how to add, how to multiply, or how to write an essay. Once a plan is developed it can be applied to similar situations. For instance, once we have learned to tie a knot in string we can tie similar knots to join laces, cotton, rope, wire or even strips of paper. In this respect plans are essential to our efficient existence. Once formed, a plan can be used over and over again, and so saves the solving of every problem from the beginning. However, like many good and useful things, a plan is a good servant but a bad master, because the use of existing plans may hinder creative thought.

The limiting effect of set in the use of plans   Although the application of previously determined plans to related new problem situations is usually advantageous, there is the risk that their employment may hinder flexible thinking. Luchins (1942) demonstrated the unhelpful aspect of plans when subjects become *set* in their application. Subjects were given eleven problems of obtaining exact quantities of water from an unlimited supply using three measuring containers of stated capacities. For instance, one problem required 100 quarts to be obtained using containers A (21 quarts), B (127 quarts), and C (3 quarts). The solution was to fill B, fill A from B and to fill C twice from B, leaving 100 quarts in B. It was possible to use this solution (B–A–2C) for problems 2-8, 10 and 11. However, a much simpler solution of items 5, 7, 8, 9, 10 and 11 was to use only two containers (A and C). For instance, problem 11 was to obtain 6 quarts using A (14 quarts), B (36 quarts) and C (8 quarts). Although B–A–2C will do, A–C is a much more economical solution.

Luchins found that subjects experienced set in that they continued to solve the items having the short solution using the long method they had devised for the first few problems. The set even persisted for some subjects after they had done item 9 which could only be solved by A–C. (In an informal replication with a group of twenty-three college of education students, 78 per cent used the long solution for item eleven!)

Set in children   In a study of set in children, Cunningham (1965) used a slightly modified version of the water-jar test already described and an alphabet maze test, with groups of seven- and eleven-year-olds. He found results similar to those using older subjects. In general, he concluded that susceptibility to set and ability to overcome set were not influenced by age, intelligence or sex to any marked extent. In the study, some subjects were allowed to use actual water and jars while others did the pencil and paper version of the test. Although subjects using real materials tended to overcome set more easily than those that did not, the difference was not significant. Stress, induced by giving a difficult test before the main session, did increase susceptibility to set.

A flexible thinker is one who can approach a problem bearing in mind the available relevant plans, but who can devise a new and more efficient plan if the situation allows it. There is the well known story of the six-year-old child who was asked by his teacher to find the sum of $1+2+3+4+5+6+7+8+9+10$. While his fellow pupils were adding $1+2=3$, $3+3=6$, and so on, applying the usual plan of addition, this child considered the problem for a moment and then wrote down the answer, 55. How did he do it?, the teacher enquired. The child explained that the numbers could be paired from the ends ($1+10=11$, $2+9=11$, etc.) to give five pairs, $5 \times 11 = 55$. The child was Gauss, who grew up to be a great mathematician.

PROBLEM SOLVING AND MOTIVATION

It is a common experience that solving problems fosters motivation and brings pleasure. Many school staff rooms have their groups of cross-word addicts who spend their morning breaks solving the puzzle in their favourite paper. Inventors and researchers often become so involved in the problem they are trying to solve that they can think of nothing else. Archimedes is reputed to have been so overjoyed at his discovery at the local baths of the principle of flotation, that he ran home without his clothes shouting 'Eureka'! Finding out can be fun, but it is only fun if there is just the right level of difficulty for the children.

Harter (1974) studied the relationship between the amount of pleasure gained from problem solving and the relative difficulty of the task. Pleasure is obviously hard to measure. She noted how much pupils smiled while solving the problems by grading it on a four point scale; no smile, 0; slight or half smile, 1; full smile or grin, 2; laugh or giggle, 3. She gave ten- and eleven-year-old children anagrams to solve. She found that the children gained more pleasure from correct than incorrect items, and that on the correctly solved anagrams the more difficult the problem the greater the smiling. When correctly solved problems were presented a second time there was a decline in smiling.

FACILITATING PRODUCTIVE THINKING

Consideration of the pattern of productive thinking given in figure 6.1 indicates that when a child is faced with a problem he goes through three stages in solving it:

1 The *recognition of the problem* to be solved — the child wanting the biscuits realises that there is possibly a way of reaching them.

2 The *production of a plan* to solve the problem — the youngster had to work out how to get the biscuits.

3 An *evaluation* of how efficient the plan is, or, in the case of other tasks, how good the product is.

Training in productive thinking will need to improve performance in these three areas. To begin with, children need to be made alert to recognise potential problems. Consider young Gauss; he recognised that in the addition task there was more than one method of finding the answer. A child who is going to discover or to be creative is one who is questioning. He will ask himself, 'Can I write a better essay by altering the structure?' or 'Will I be able to make a better picture by using different materials?', or 'Is it possible to measure the length of the playground more efficiently using another instrument?' Pupils need to be shown that there are often several ways of doing things, and encouraged to recognise potential problems and to question existing methods.

A study of the improvement of creative thinking by the training of the production and evaluation of ideas has been made by Stratton and Brown (1972). As problem tasks they asked four groups of undergraduate subjects to suggest titles for a story plot. All subjects had two plot–title problems. Between the pre- and post-test, group one received a production training programme, group two a judgement training programme, group three both programmes, and group four a filler task unrelated to the problems.

The production training programme was intended to improve the quantity of ideas generated, and was based on the pretraining material. Subjects were instructed how to construct an idea table in which the plot was divided into sections and related information listed under each section. The last part of the training was to apply to the passage, the method that would be used in the final test. The judgement training aimed at improving the quality of decisions about how good ideas were, and was also based on the pretraining plot and solutions. The programme consisted of a description of how plot titles might be rated. Examples were given of good and poor titles and subjects practised choosing the best titles out of a given set. The combined training consisted of both the production and judgement programmes. The changes in performance from pre- to post-test are given in figure 6.2. It was found that production

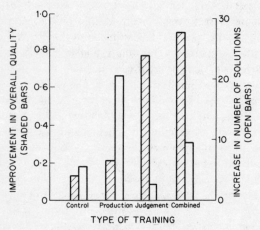

Figure 6.2 Changes in production and quality performance (adapted from Stratton and Brown 1972)

training helped production but not quality, while judgement training improved quality but not quantity, which was in fact reduced relative to the control group. The best all round performance was from the combined training group. A further finding was that the least able subjects, as assessed by the pre-test, showed the greatest improvement.

This study points to both the need for, and effectiveness of, training in the judgement of the quality of ideas and plans as well as in their production. It is necessary for the teacher to maintain a balance.

CONCLUSIONS ABOUT PRODUCTIVE THINKING

The experimental evidence that is available suggests that children cannot be creative out of nothing. New creations are the combination in a new way of what they already know or have experienced. The pupil who has a very restricted vocabulary is not going to produce a piece of brilliant creative writing however much he is stimulated, because he has not the necessary terms in which to express himself. The child who has little understanding of measuring instruments and principles is unlikely to be the one who suggests a novel method of determining the length of the playground. People who have made radical departures into new forms of art or music have usually been very competent at the traditional forms first. The implication for the teacher of this dependence of creation on existing knowledge is that children must internalise information if they are to think productively with it.

Having stressed the need for knowledge and experience to be available for critical thinking to take place, it must also be said that productive thinking needs to be fostered and encouraged. This is particularly so in the case of children with a very deprived home background where there is little stimulation to think and where questions are ignored so that the child's natural inquisitiveness is starved. It is also necessary in the case of the child from an overly strict home where the child's questioning is discouraged and his natural creativeness squashed. (An unthinking teacher or a severely strict teacher can produce the same effect given time.) Children will need practise in producing ideas and plans, and in evaluating them. In this respect discovery learning can provide useful experience.

Methods of learning: reception and discovery

We may learn either by being given information in a form that is ready for our minds to receive, or by discovering the information for ourselves. Suppose you are asked to convert fifty-two degrees Fahrenheit into degrees Centigrade. Assuming your present ignorance of the method, you are faced with a choice; you can either look up the method in a book, or puzzle out the problem of temperature scales on your own. Here are two different means of acquiring information. The first is *reception learning*, where the material is given in a form that is ready to receive, and the second is *discovery learning*, which entails two stages: (a) the discovery of the information by reasoning or experimentation and (b) the learning of the information discovered. Ausubel (1968, chapter 14) pointed out that discovery learning almost amounts to reception learning plus a preceding problem stage.

During the past few years there has been considerable controversy over the merits of these methods of learning. On the one hand, Bruner (1961) and others have argued that discovery learning is superior to reception learning. On the other, Ausubel has challenged this view and defended reception learning. Before the experimental evidence is considered, it is necessary to clarify what is meant by discovery learning in the school context.

Degrees of guidance in learning   In practice, although opposing opinions tend to polarise our view, there are obviously degrees of guidance possible in learning which range from pure discovery to complete guidance. In the learning of the principles of balance mentioned at the beginning of this chapter, the teacher could either give the pupils the equipment (metre rod, weights, wedge, etc) and tell them to find out the rules of balance and leave them to their own devices, or having given them the equipment he could direct their investigations and help them when they get stuck, or he could give them the equipment and demonstrate the rules and get them to try them out for themselves. These three degrees of guidance may be shown in a diagram:

PURE DISCOVERY   GUIDED DISCOVERY   RECEPTION

Increasing amount of direction from the teacher

Pure discovery is when no assistance, other than encouragement, is given by the teacher. In guided discovery a degree of aid is given; for instance, when a child gets stuck, another approach to the problem is suggested for him to try. Reception learning is when the pupil is highly directed with maximal help from the teacher; there is little actual discovery by the student. In real school learning the extremes must be very rare. Further, many learning situations which claim to be discovery orientated are not really so in the sense of problem solving. For instance, much topic work in which children 'have to find out for themselves' often only require pupils to choose a book on the topic and to work from it in a reception learning fashion.

The distinction between guidance and concrete activity   In the past, discovery learning has been associated with children being allowed to actively handle materials, whereas reception learning has often been linked to pupils sitting in rows facing a blackboard in a highly formal teaching situation. This view confuses the issue. Discovery learning refers to the amount of guidance a pupil is given in learning and not to the amount of concrete activity. A child can be equally active in using concrete objects and in other learning activities in reception learning, as he can in discovery learning. Thus the term 'activity method' is not synonymous with 'discovery method'.

The claims for discovery learning   It has already been noted that Bruner has been one of the leading advocates of the discovery method. He has argued (1961) that learning through discovery has four advantages over the reception method. He lists these as, '(1) The increase in intellectual potency, (2) the shift from extrinsic to intrinsic rewards, (3) learning the heuristics of discovering, and (4) the aid to memory processing'. Ausubel, on the other hand, has stressed that the value of reception learning is underrated and the teaching of discovery skills is not always appropriate to children.

EXPERIMENTAL WORK ON DISCOVERY LEARNING
When learning methods are compared there are often so many variables to be taken into account that clearcut results are

difficult to obtain. This is particularly so in the case of reception and discovery learning, where the relevant variables might include the age and ability of the pupils, the type of material to be learned, the time available to learn it, the nature of the measure of what is learned, and the period for which information must be remembered. To control for and systematically manipulate all of these variables is far from easy. A selection of studies will be considered. The reader is invited to pose the question, 'Which learning method is best and under what conditions?', and critically to examine the results of each study and to determine how effectively the variables were controlled.

Learning to use a micrometer (*fourteen-year-olds*)   Ray (1961) compared pupil discovery with direct instruction. The learning task was the use of a precision measuring instrument, the micrometer calliper. Subjects were taught the names of the parts of the instrument and their functions, and how to use the micrometer to make measurements. The subjects were divided into high, medium and low ability levels, and then randomly allocated to two experimental groups and one control group. One experimental group received direct instruction and the other directed discovery. The control group received no instruction. Care was taken to ensure that in other respects the subjects were treated in the same manner. Subjects in the experimental groups were taught in groups of nine with three from each of the ability levels. The instruction-learning period was 47 minutes long, and the same introductory material was given to both groups for the first seven minutes. To ensure that the conditions were the same for all subgroups the instructions were tape recorded and the illustrations put on slides.

The direct instruction group were presented with the material by the teacher, who emphasised the main points and worked through some examples. The teacher spoke all the time. By contrast, the directed discovery group were encouraged to be active, and each pupil studied the illustrations on his own and considered questions posed by the teacher. For almost half the time the teacher was silent while the subjects discovered the principles and made generalisations.

Learning performance was measured in two ways:

1 *Retention* was tested by subjects measuring the sizes of blocks and then doing paper and pencil items to demonstrate their knowledge of the use of the gauge.

2 The ability to *transfer* the knowledge to new but related situations was also assessed with performance and written tests.

The retention tests were given immediately after the instruction and again after one week and six weeks. Transfer was measured after one week and then after six. A simplified form of the results is given in table 6.3. The direct teaching group did best on immediate recall, while the directed discovery subjects were superior after six weeks on both retention and transfer. The methods were equally appropriate for all of the ability levels.

Table 6.3 Retention and transfer scores for groups

(adapted from Ray 1961)

Group	Retention		Transfer
	Immediate	After 6 weeks	After 6 weeks
Reception	51	45	14
Discovery	46	49	20

Learning mathematical rules about a number series Kersh (1962), working with American high school students found over a six week retention interval that the application of rules about the addition of number series was better with a rote learning group than with guided discovery or directed reception groups who learned explanations of the rules. Retention of the rules, however, was best by the guided discovery group. Kersh attributed this latter superiority of the guided discovery method to the enhanced motivation of the group who were more personally involved. However, since the discovery method was not typical of the everyday experience of the students, it may well be that it was the novelty of the method rather than the method itself that produced the result.

Meconi (1967) compared pure discovery, guided discovery and reception methods of learning mathematical concepts by thirteen- and fourteen-year-old pupils. He found little difference between the methods in problem solving and retention performance, and concluded that what is learned is more important than how it is learned.

Learning a language code (*postgraduate students*)   Rowell, Simon and Wiseman (1969) allocated postgraduate subjects to two experimental groups: guided discovery and verbal reception method. The material to be learned was equally unfamiliar to all subjects and consisted of seventeen symbols, each associated with a separate meaning. New meanings could be produced by the combination of symbols. For example, a rectangle meant 'container' and an arrow meant 'moves', so a rectangle with an arrow below it represented 'vehicle'. The *verbal reception group* were shown the symbols and their meanings and heard a short lecture in which examples of building up new meanings were given, followed by fifteen minutes to learn the basic symbols and the examples, and to practise building more complex groups. Afterwards all notes were collected from the subjects. The *guided discovery group* were given examples of new meanings and asked to discover from them the individual meanings of the basic symbols and the rules for building up new meanings. They were also instructed that when they had found these meanings they were to learn them and the examples of symbol combinations and to practise writing new combinations. The subjects discovered by question and answer and all completed within the fourteen minutes, the same time as the reception group's lecture.

The learning was followed by tests after half an hour, after one week and after ten weeks. Each test required recall of the meanings of the seventeen basic symbols and the fourteen examples. This was followed by an application section which required five meanings to be translated into symbols and five symbols to be translated into meanings. The verbal reception group did significantly better on all three tests of both application and recall. For example, after ten weeks the application scores for the reception and discovery groups were, respectively, 5·8 and 4·6 out of 10, and for retention, 23·5 and 20·3 out of 31.

CHOICE OF LEARNING METHOD

So far the experimental work on the merits of the methods of learning is difficult to generalise. Little attention has been paid to some variables that are of particular interest to the teacher. For instance, age differences have not been studied, particularly in relation to Piaget's stages of the development of thinking, nor has the effect of the amount of guidance. Further, the differences in performance between the experimental groups is usually relatively small, so that in practice no one method could be claimed to be superior.

In terms of the *quality of learning* there is probably no difference in the understanding produced by either reception or guided discovery learning. This is particularly true when equal times are allowed for the two methods, since discovery requires much time and if this were devoted to good reception learning the degree of understanding achieved by the reception method would probably be very high. It must also be noted that the discovery method can lead to poor, meaningless learning when it is possible for the pupil to discover the answers to questions without seeing why or how.

There is, on the whole, no evidence that discovery produces better *retention* of what is learned than reception, although, as Kersh observed, there is likely to be an interaction between retention and motivation. It has been noted already that care must be taken to control for a novelty effect when using the discovery method with children for whom it is new. Since variety is a considerable aid to *motivation*, a careful combination of reception and discovery methods will best maintain interest. In discovery learning, motivation will only be kept up if the pupil meets with reasonable success. If he continually fails to make headway he will become frustrated and lose interest. The judicious use of guidance is very important. Too little guidance leads to boredom; too much robs the pupil of the joy of discovery. Herman (1969), who made a careful survey of work on discovery learning, concluded that the degree of guidance is one of the key factors determining the effectiveness of discovery methods.

Discovery learning of both the pure and guided types provides useful experience for pupils in *critical thinking* and problem solving. It may be that, on average, discovery produces slightly better transfer to new situations. The choice of learning method should depend much more on a consideration of the objectives chosen for a topic and on the teaching strategy adopted, than on one method being innately superior to the other.

TO THINK ABOUT

1 List five plans that pupils learn at school.

2 How is it possible to encourage children to avoid set in the application of plans?

3 How does the idea of 'available functions' affect your view of a child's creative response to a stimulus situation?

4 Is flexible thinking in all children a worthwhile educational objective?

5 Devise a short training programme that would encourage pupils of a given age to recognise problems, and produce and evaluate plans.

6 Plan in outline both a reception and a discovery method by which a given topic might be learned.

7 For which age groups, abilities of pupils and subject matter areas is the discovery approach most suitable?

7

Styles of learning

Individual differences

When you walk into a school, the first thing you notice is children, the second is that they all look different! They vary in sex, size and colouring. After a little time with the children you also find that they differ very much in abilities and interests too. Some readily understand what you say while others seem slow to comprehend. Some children are very talkative while their companions are shy and retiring. In earlier chapters, where the basic processes of learning were considered, the similarity between people was stressed in order to determine general rules about learning. In the present chapter some of the ways in which children differ in the manner in which they learn will be considered.

Recent research into the ways in which pupils learn and represent information in memory suggests that, if children are to gain the maximum amount of benefit from education, account must be taken of their different ways of learning. A child who functions differently from his teacher may be thought by the teacher to be dull, while another who has the same overall ability but who fits into the teacher's style may be considered brighter than he really is.

In this chapter, two aspects of individual style will be discussed. The first is how outgoing and how stable the child is in his personality. The second concerns the way in which the learner represents information in memory. It is likely that these two aspects are to some degree related, but for simplicity they will be considered separately.

Personality and learning style

Eysenck (1960) has suggested that a person's personality can be expressed in terms of two dimensions of behaviour. These dimensions are how socially outgoing the person is, how *extraverted*, and how *neurotic* he is. Consider the extraversion dimension; a person may be very outgoing, happy in the company of strangers, lively, social, never lacking for conversation. By contrast another may be just the opposite, inward, shy in the company of people he does not know, usually quiet, an *introvert*. Similarly on the neuroticism dimension, an individual may be calm, relaxed, not easily ruffled, able to cope with life, very *stable*, while another is at the other extreme — frequently anxious, often feeling nervous, not very secure, unsure of himself, *neurotic*. An individual may be at any point on each dimension.

Eysenck and Eysenck (1964) have developed a test to determine an individual's degree of extraversion and neuroticism, and this has been adapted by Sybil Eysenck (1965) as the Junior Eysenck Personality Inventory for use with children. Briefly, the test consists of questions which assess how children react to social and anxiety producing situations. Examples of the style of the questions (although not actual items from the test) are: 'Do you like playing at the homes of other children?', to which an extravert will answer 'Yes' but which an introvert may be less happy about. A question like, 'Are you very frightened in the dark?', when answered affirmatively, may indicate a tendency to be neurotic. There are twenty-four questions for each personality dimension, and these are randomly ordered in the test. Analysis of the answers to the questions allows the degree of extraversion and neuroticism to be found for a child.

The effect of personality on two aspects of school learning will be considered.

1 PERSONALITY AND OVERALL ATTAINMENT

An initial question is whether personality affects overall attainment in school subjects. The short answer is that studies have not found any dramatic relationship. The overall trend is that extraverts do better when they are young but that the picture changes as children get older and after about fourteen years introverts tend to have the higher attainment. With neuroticism, there appears to be no overall relationship. In order to put these general statements into context, two studies of personality and attainment will be described.

In a study of approximately 110 eight-year-old children Elliott (1972) gave the Junior Eysenck Personality Inventory, the Moray House Picture Intelligence Test, and the Schonell Graded Word Recognition Test.

Table 7.1   Correlation of attainment at eight years

(adapted from Elliott 1972)

	Reading age	Intelligence
Extraversion	0·60	0·43
Neuroticism	−0·59	−0·29

Personality and attainment were compared by determining the correlation coefficients. The results are given in table 7.1. (A perfect correlation has a value of one or minus one; zero indicates no relationship.) He found that reading was positively related to extraversion, that is, the more outgoing a child is the higher attainment is likely to be. Introverted children tended to have a lower reading age. In the case of neuroticism, a negative correlation with reading performance was found. This meant that neurotic children did not do so well at reading as their more stable fellows. Although these results suggest a fairly clear relationship between personality and reading attainment, a study by Savage (1966) with children of almost the same age found much smaller correlations between the Watts Sentence Reading Test and extraversion and neuroticism (0·19 and −0·22 respectively).

Eysenck and Cookson (1969) tested 4,000 eleven-year-old primary school children on the Junior Eysenck Personality Inventory, tests of verbal reasoning, mathematics and English attainment, and the Schonell Graded Word Reading Test. The approximate correlations between extraversion, neuroticism and attainment are given in table 7.2. The results were very similar for both boys and girls:

Table 7.2   **Personality and attainment at eleven years**

(adapted from Eysenck and Cookson 1969)

	Reading	Reasoning	Maths	English
Extraversion	0·23	0·19	0·20	0·19
Neuroticism	−0·06	−0·11	−0·11	−0·10

Inspection of the correlations indicates that they are all considerably lower than those found by Elliott for eight-year-olds. While at eleven extraverts and stable pupils perform slightly better than introverts and neurotics, the correlations are so small that it is unlikely that the teacher will notice the difference. A correlation coefficient of 0·20 means that only 4 per cent of the variation in children's performance is due to the personality variable.

While more studies are required to complete the picture the approximate overall trend in the relationship between extraversion and attainment is given in table 7.3.

Table 7.3   **Approximate change in the relationship between extraversion and attainment with age**

(based on Elliott 1972)

Age (years)	7-8	11-12	13-14	15-16	18-19
Correlation	0·40	0·14	−0·05	−0·08	−0·50

The correlations given are very tentative and are based on comparatively few studies, but they indicate the general shift from superiority by the extraverted children when they are young, to better performance by introverts at the secondary level. The changeover appears to take place at about thirteen years.

With regard to neuroticism the trend is less clear. This is

partly because the relationship between anxiety and performance is more complex. In a study with two age groups, Leith and Davis (1972) found a humped relationship between neuroticism and performance. Twelve-and-a-half-year-olds and thirteen-and-a-half-year-olds worked through five programmes typical of a range of school work (e.g. the structure of language, the formation of V-shaped valleys, mathematical sets, etc) each taking about fifty minutes. Their mean achievement scores on these topics according to their neuroticism level is given in table 7.4.

Table 7.4 **Approximate mean achievement score on programme**
(adapted from Leith and Davis 1972)

Age (years)	Neuroticism level		
	low	average	high
12·5	42	50	50
13·5	49	54	49

Look at the scores for the thirteen-and-a-half-year-olds. The children who performed best were those who had an average amount of anxiety. Those who were very stable (i.e. a low level of neuroticism) were probably less anxious to succeed, while the very neurotic pupils were likely to have been hampered by their nervousness. In other words the most successful children at this age are those who have some anxiety, but not too much.

Leith and Davis chose these two age groups because they suspected that they covered a critical age at which the effect of anxiety changes. Consider the younger group. In their case the presence of high anxiety does not have a deleterious effect. The performance is the same for high as it is for average neuroticism. They concluded that in children below about thirteen years anxiety facilitates school achievement, whereas above that age it reduces performance. The alert reader will have noticed that this view does not agree with the finding of Elliott mentioned earlier, that reading performance correlates negatively with neuroticism for young children. The discrepancy between these findings indicates the complexity of research in this area. A basic problem is that anxiety probably does not affect all types of school work in the same way. Further, an anxious child may well perform quite well on a programme that he can work through by himself at his own pace, but feel very different if he has to read aloud to the teacher in a test. When interpreting research findings, the teacher must guard against generalising conclusions from one situation to others that are different.

As a general rule it is likely that a child's performance on a task will be best when he has some interest in his success but not too much, since if he is too worried it will interfere with actual performance even though he really wants to succeed.

At present, the overall picture of the effect of personality on school achievement is not very clear. Entwistle (1972) has pointed out the need for more studies and for more careful control of their design. One of the problems has been that the same type of attainment tests has not been used in all studies. Further, the lack of any dramatic relationship between personality and attainment may be because most of the studies have used large samples of children who have come from different schools having different teachers and a variety of teaching methods. This will have tended to mask any personality effects that were present. In the following sections the relation between personality and learning in more specific situations will be considered. In particular, the effect of the structure of the learning material and of individual versus group learning will be reviewed.

2 PERSONALITY AND THE STRUCTURE OF THE LEARNING TASK

The experienced teacher will have observed that children differ in the way in which they can cope with different types of learning tasks. Even those new to teaching will probably have noticed that, when attending lectures at college, they reacted differently from some of their friends in the way they were able to assimilate the material. Some students would have been very sensitive to the logical structure of the material and would have found handouts giving the outline of the lecture useful aids to the reception of that material, while others would have found that the structuring of the material neither helped nor hindered their understanding.

These casual observations point to a potentially important area of difference in learning. Work on personality and the structure of the learning task suggest that introverts differ from extraverts in the structures that they find easiest to learn. Generally it appears that introverts are helped when the structure of the material is clearly given. Extraverts, on the other hand, are less concerned about the structure and if anything prefer some contact with the material before being given its logical structure.

Leith and Trown (1970), in a study with twelve-year-olds, compared giving mathematical rules before practice at examples, with presenting the rules after the practice. Over a four-week period the children worked through a new mathematics programme which contained sixteen rules, each of which was exemplified in exercises and problems. One group of children received the rule before each set of problems while the other had the rule after the set. At the end of the four weeks all subjects were given a test of their knowledge of the material and a transfer test of new items. The mean scores on the tests for extraverts and introverts are given in table 7.5.

Table 7.5 Mean scores on knowledge and transfer tests
(adapted from Leith and Trown 1970)

Test	Personality	Position of rules	
		Before practice	After practice
Knowledge	Introvert	55	53
	Extravert	43	55
Transfer	Introvert	40	37
	Extravert	25	43

The results indicate that extraverts and introverts differ in their preferred order of the material. Although the trend was not very strong, introverts found that they performed best when the rule introduced each section and gave them the conceptual structure of the subject matter, whereas the extraverts did much better when the rules followed the problems.

In another study of the effect of structure, Leith (1973) contrasted learning from material presented in small logical steps with the presentation of large steps. Twelve-year-old children studied programmes on rain fall over a five-week period and then completed a thirty-six item test. The performance on the test is indicated in table 7.6.

Table 7.6   Effect of step size and extraversion on learning
(adapted from Leith 1973)

Personality	Test Score for Programme step size	
	Large	Small
Introvert	17	24
Extravert	20	19

Here the introverts performed best when the structure was clearly given in small units, while the more outgoing children showed little preference.

It appears, then, that introverts are happier when the logical structure of the learning material is clear for them to see. Extraverts, on the other hand, are not helped by structure and if anything prefer the structure after some familiarity with the material. An obvious question concerns why this should be. While a complete answer is not possible at this stage, it is likely that introverts and extraverts organise information differently in memory. Some evidence for this view comes from a study by Eysenck and Howarth (1968), who found that with student subjects extreme extraverts differed from extreme introverts in their ability to recall a list of pairs of nonsense syllables. All subjects learned the list of fourteen syllables to a criterion of one correct recall. The extraverts recalled better than introverts on the immediate recall of the list, having a mean of twelve syllables, but became poorer after one day when they dropped to seven.

The introverts only managed to remember seven immediately but the group recalling after a day had eleven. Certainly, these results indicate that different changes in the availability of information recall takes place in the two personality groups.

Further support for the notion that personality affects the memory structure was found in an experiment by Jones (1976), in which the extent to which children integrated recently received related information into a whole was investigated. The biographical details of the life of an explorer were put into chronological order and then divided alternately into two sets so that a pair of different passages about the person's life were constructed. Twelve-year-old children heard one of the passages followed immediately by the second passage. Immediately and after one hour different groups of the children were asked to write down all the details they could recall from the first passage, but not to give any of the details from the second. It was expected that the introverted subjects would integrate the two highly related passages in memory because by so doing they would form a much more logical structure. While the extraverts would be content to retain the two forms of the biography separately. Further, it was expected that the longer the subjects retained the information the more pronounced the effect would be. The percentage of details recalled by introverts from the second passage in error was therefore expected to exceed that recalled by the extraverts. The results are shown in table 7.7.

Table 7.7 Items recalled from first passage as a percentage of total recall

Personality	Retention interval (mins)	
	0	60
Introvert	86	64
Extravert	86	89

The results show that while there was no difference at immediate recall, the introverted subjects later tended to integrate the two passages and, as time went on, they found it increasingly difficult to separate them. The extraverts showed no such trend but appeared to keep the two parts of the material separate in memory.

Although much research is needed to determine the exact relationships between extraversion and learning, it is clear that individual differences in this personality dimension are responsible for quite distinct approaches to learning by children.

The degree of neuroticism also has an effect on learning performance in that anxious children seem to prefer well structured learning tasks where what they have to do is quite clear. However, the effect of neuroticism is subject to greater variation than extraversion because a child's anxiety will also depend on the stressfulness of the situation, the amount of approval from the teacher and his age. The degree of structure that produces the best results for a child is therefore not constant. This is demonstrated by the conflicting findings of different studies. For instance, Leith and Bossett (1967) noted that anxious ten-year-olds performed best when provided with a completely structured learning material, while Tallmadge and Shearer (1971) found that the achievement was highest when there was an element of discovery and thinking out the structure in the task. It is evident that the teacher must make a judgement in each learning situation. If pupils learn best when the level of arousal or anxiety is moderate, then the teacher will need to reduce the stress on a very anxious child when the task is not structured. This will probably be best accomplished by giving approval and reassurance.

Learning and memory form

A second area of individual variation concerns the manner in which information is represented in memory. Consider the sentence, 'On a warm afternoon in late summer the village children were playing on the green in the shade of an old beech tree.' As you read those words you automatically analysed their meaning and determined the sense of the whole sentence. While this will be so for all readers, the form in which the sense was stored in memory will depend on the individual. There are two basic ways of representing the meaning of information, verbal and visual. How did you, the reader, code the meaning? Did you do it verbally in terms of the association or word meaning, or was it in the form of a picture of the scene on the village green? Since you carried out your analysis automatically you may have to think carefully about the form in which you code information. It may, in fact, be in both forms simultaneously.

Discussions about prose comprehension with both adults and children suggest that some people experience pictures or visual imagery much more than others. Indeed, some individuals report that even when listening to, say, a story, they do not have any images at all. These casual observations indicate a considerable variation in the occurrence and use of imagery by learners. The teacher will be interested to inquire whether the way a child represents information in memory affects his learning performance. Although this is an area of research that has only begun to be tackled in recent years, the answer appears to be that it does. However, work on the representation of information in memory poses difficult problems for the investigator, and it is as well to consider these first.

The fundamental problem in considering the memory code that children use, or prefer to use, is in determining what the form of representation actually is. When you read the sentence about the children playing on the village green, you analysed it so quickly that you hardly noticed the form you used. Since people are not very clear about the way they represent meaning and since the experimenter cannot look inside their minds to find out, indirect methods of assessment must be used. Three general approaches to the determination of the memory code have been tried. While each has some limitation, it is important to add that all have been successful in discriminating between differences in performance on actual learning tasks. The three methods are, (a) the introspective report of imagery vividness, (b) tests of spatial ability, and (c) the measurement of the response time necessary to generate an image. Each of these methods will be described, together with a study using the method to group learners into verbal and visual code groups to compare their learning performance.

In the *introspective report method* subjects are asked to visualise objects and to rate the vividness of image they obtain. Think of an empty cup on a saucer, now think of it full of coffee. Do you have a vivid image, a clear picture? An obvious difficulty is that what one person considers vivid, another may not. Further, a subject may say he has a vivid picture of the object because he thinks that by so doing he will please or impress the experimenter. Despite these difficulties, Marks (1973) found that subjects who reported vivid images when asked to think about a series of objects were better at recalling the content of coloured photographs than subjects who said they did not have clear images. This suggests that images are important in memory, and that some people find it easier than others to form them.

The second approach is *to measure spatial ability* on the assumption that imagers, or visualisers, are better at solving spatial tasks than verbalisers. Typically, spatial ability is measured in terms of how quickly a subject can rearrange a set of coloured wooden blocks to produce a given pattern, or how well a shape or pattern that is given can be found in a series of very similar ones containing the shape, or how fast a set of cardboard shapes can be fitted together to form, say, a square. Although it would be better to be able to measure imagery directly, rather than its correlate, this method has been successfully used with children.

Hollenberg (1970) divided six- to ten-year-old children into high- and low-imagery groups on the basis of their performance on a battery of spatial ability tests. She used what amounted to two learning tasks. In the first, the children saw four pictures each of which had a new word attached to it. The words were 'pog', 'nad', 'tus' and 'jek' and their respective pictures were of food, a toy, a small-headed creature and a fat-headed creature. The series of pictures were presented one at a time with their 'name' until the child could correctly give the name for each picture. It was expected that in this task the visualisers (high imagery ability) would learn more quickly than the verbalisers (low imagery ability) because they would find it easier to form an image of the item and to label it. This was found to be so, the visualisers learned the names in only four presentations while the verbalisers needed an average of six.

The second learning task was an extension of the first but required the children to be able to abstract common features from additional pictures in order to attain new concepts. The subjects were presented with several series of new pictures and asked to say which of the names they had learned best fitted what they saw. The new pictures each depicted a new example of the items on the original series. For instance, the original food picture, 'pog', showed a pear, while the next showed an ice-cream cone, and the others showed a loaf of bread, cherries, a pie, a banana, and so on. As each new picture was presented the child guessed the correct name which, if wrong, was given by the experimenter. With this task it was anticipated that the verbalisers would learn the concepts more quickly because the visualisers would tend to find that the exact image of each item would dominate their thinking, so that they would be hindered in extracting the general principle behind each of the new words. The results of the study supported this view. The visualisers took an average of six showings of each concept to learn it, while the verbalisers only required four, although the difference in performance became less pronounced as the children got older. The findings of this study indicate that there are differences in the way in which primary school children process information and store it in memory and that these differences can affect their learning performance.

In the third method, the *time subjects take to form images* is measured. Subjects are asked to visualise an object in response to its name and to press a button when they have done so. This approach was used by early workers in this field and more recently by Paivio and his co-workers. For instance, Ernest and Paivio (1971) showed that subjects who did well on spatial ability tests were able to form images in response to noun stimuli more quickly than those of lower spatial ability.

An adaptation of the response time method has been used to

attempt to assess the type of memory code employed by children when analysing prose material (Riding and Taylor 1976). If it is assumed that some children use a predominantly imaginal form while others store new information in a verbal form, then it should be possible to distinguish between them on the basis of the speed of their response to a question about the prose material. For instance, if the following sentences were read to a child, 'The little boy walked slowly up the cobbled path to the old cottage. When he reached the door he paused and looked at it before knocking' and then the question, 'What colour was the door?' then those who used imaginal coding would have translated what they heard into a visualisation of the scene and consequently would have been able to reply very quickly with the colour of the door which they could 'see'. By contrast, children who coded information in purely verbal form would not have the image and when asked the question would have to search memory for possible colours of doors and select one in order to reply; a process which would take longer than using an image. The coding style used could therefore be inferred from the time taken to respond, fast responders would be imagers while the slower ones would be verbalisers. Obviously, between these extremes there will be children who use dual coding (i.e. both visual and verbal), although it is likely that one mode will still be stronger or more complete than the other.

In the study by Riding and Taylor, seven-year-old year old children were given a test to determine their dominant form of memory code. This consisted of a short story divided into ten paragraphs. After each paragraph a question was inserted requiring information that a listener could add to each paragraph if an image of the incident described was formed, but which could not be answered directly from the paragraph, rather like the example about the cottage door. The children's response times to the questions were recorded. On subsequent days the children listened to two prose passages, one having concrete and the other more abstract content. Examples of sentences from the concrete and abstract passages were, respectively, 'A small brown mouse came out of his hole, and crossed the room so that he could explore the Christmas tree,' and 'Long ago, in the land of Chen, which is far away in the eastern half of the world, there lived a princess called Lo-Yen.' The intention was that the concrete passage should permit the listener to readily generate images of the events, while the abstract passage would tend to allow only verbal coding. Both passages were appropriate for young children and were very similar in word difficulty as indicated by word-frequency count scores. After each passage the subjects received a ten question comprehension test.

On the basis of their mean response times to the imagery test questions subjects were divided into three groups. It has been argued that a low response time would be indicative of imaginal coding of information whereas slow would reflect predominantly verbal coding. The three groups were therefore designated high, medium and low imagery in the order in which their response times increased. The comprehension test scores for the three groups on the concrete and abstract passages are given in table 7.8.

Table 7.8 Comprehension scores and imagery performance
(adapted from Riding and Taylor 1976)

Passage type	Imagery performance on memory code test		
	high	medium	low
Concrete	8·8	6·8	3·5
Abstract	5·5	5·6	7·1

As might be expected, the better the imagery test performance the higher the score on the concrete passage. What was of particular interest was that the low imagery group performed best on abstract material. It appears that the imagers tend to be poor at verbal coding and vice versa.

Although it is too early to be sure about the interpretation of these results they do suggest that infant school children differ in their ability to learn concrete and abstract prose. Inspection of the comprehension test scores showed that most children did considerably better on one passage than on the other, and that the preference was roughly equally divided.

CONCLUSIONS

In discussing the research into the distinction between visualisers and verbalisers, the point has been stressed that the work is still at an early stage, and consequently many problems await solution. There are at least two basic difficulties. The first is knowing exactly what role visual images play in the learner's understanding of information. In the preceding reviews the assumption has been that they are a means of representing meaning in memory, but further research may show that they are only incidental, a sort of optional extra. The second difficulty is being sure measures of coding differences actually assess coding and not some other ability.

Despite these uncertainties the measures of imagery performance do appear to be tapping some important underlying difference in the manner in which people process information. Even if further studies show that the present descriptions are not entirely correct, the picture is clear enough to indicate that these differences in performance warrant a teacher's attention.

From a school point of view, inspection of table 7.8 clearly shows that there was little difference in *overall* performance between the visualisers and verbalisers when the results for the two passages were combined. The implication of this will be that with a variety of learning materials children of both types appear equally able. However, if a child who is a visualiser consistently receives abstract material, then he will appear dull compared with his verbaliser counterpart.

RELATION BETWEEN PERSONALITY AND MEMORY CODE

An important question is whether personality and the learner's dominant memory code are related. A study by Huckabee (1974) suggests introverts tend to be visualisers while extraverts are verbalisers. Using the introspective report method of assessing imagery, he asked students to rate the ease with which lists of abstract and concrete nouns evoked images. These ratings were compared with extraversion scores from the Eysenck Personality Inventory. He found that introverts had higher imagery scores than extraverts, and that the difference was most pronounced for the concrete nouns.

Perceptual style

In terms of how people perceive their environment, Witkin (1962) has distinguished between those who he describes as field-dependent and those who are field-independent. His use of these terms can be best illustrated by describing a typical experiment. Each subject is seated in a dark room and sees in front of him a rod in the middle of a square frame which are both coated with luminous paint. The rod is pivoted at the centre of the frame, and it and the frame can be tilted independently of one another. In a typical trial, the subject opens his eyes to see in front of him the rod and frame, both tilted. If he perceives the rod as tilted, he is asked to turn it until it appears upright, while the frame is kept in its original position. Subjects were found to differ in that some could actually make the rod vertical while others thought it was upright when it was in line with the sides of the frame, even when it was in fact still quite tilted. Those who could make the rod vertical, independent of the frame, were termed 'field-independent' and those who could not 'field-dependent'. Witkin and his co-workers have argued that a person's degree of field-dependence affects many aspects of a person's behaviour and not just his visual perception. For instance, they have found evidence that field-dependent people prefer work that requires involvement with people, while field-independent folk are happy to work alone. Further, field-dependent children benefited from discovery learning more than field-independent pupils, perhaps because in discovery learning there is more social interaction with the teacher. Field-independent children tend to be more analytic than field-dependent ones.

What is the relationship between the field-dependence style of perceiving, and the personality and memory code dimensions already described? Although the exact connection is not clear, it is very likely that further research will show that they are all manifestations of a single variable. When one notes the parallel between perception being field-dependent and social behaviour being extravert it appears that these are simply perceptual and social manifestations of the same characteristic. Further, since the rod and frame test is basically one of spatial ability which is related to imagery, then a visual memory code and field-independence are also the memory and perceptual aspects of the same underlying attribute. At the extremes of the continuum, it is likely that people will be field-independent, introvert visualisers or dependent extravert verbalisers.

PRACTICAL CONSIDERATIONS

Three general points emerge from a consideration of research into different styles of learning.

1 The first is that there do appear to be quite marked differences in the way in which children prefer to learn and that this preference affects how efficiently they learn. Having said that, it is necessary to add the obvious point that all of the styles mentioned — personality, memory code, and field-dependence — are continuums. That is, children vary from one extreme to the other. In a class, while a few children will be extreme introverts or extraverts, most will be between these extremes. The same will apply to aspects of style.

2 While most children will be in the central portion of the distribution of learning style, many of them will still have a preferred style of learning even though it may not be very apparent to casual observation. Children who are persistently presented with information of a type and in a form that is not in keeping with their preferred style will appear considerably less able than if their style is taken into account.

3 Teachers must be on their guard against regarding their own learning style as *the* style. For instance, visualisers are likely to think that because they find pictures and diagrams an aid to understanding, the children they teach will all be helped

by a lot of visual aids. The opposite may well be the case for extreme verbalisers, who will find diagrams difficult to code.

TO THINK ABOUT

1 Can you identify, in terms of personality type, memory code and perceptual dependence, your own learning style? Do you think that styles in the three areas are the product of one basic underlying characteristic?

2 How would you plan learning for a very neurotic child so that performance is maximised?

3 To what extent is your teaching style affected by your own learning style?

4 Should learning materials and presentation methods be adapted to the individual style of the child, or should the child be encouraged to adapt to the other methods?

8

Planning learning

Planning decisions

When planning learning the teacher has to make decisions about
three aspects of the instruction. The first concerns what will be
learned and how this learning is to be evaluated. In many cases
the teacher will be guided in general terms by the syllabus, but
within this framework he will have considerable freedom to
decide on particular topics and the depth to which they are
considered. The next decision will be about the order in which
the topic or subject matter is studied. The teacher must
determine which sequence will produce the most efficient
learning. Finally, the learning activities must be considered.
For example, should the children do work cards, or should they
write about the topic in their own words?

In practice there will be considerable interaction between
these decisions. For instance, the choice of subject matter will
tend to influence both the sequencing and the learning
activities. Further, the actual decisions will obviously depend
much on the subject matter area and the age of the pupils. The
basic psychological principles behind these three areas of
decision making will therefore be considered.

Aims and evaluation

Mager (1970) took a look at trends in school learning and then
made up a fable about a sea horse who gathered up his seven
pieces of eight and set off to find his fortune. Soon he met an eel

who, for half his money, sold him a speedy flipper so that he could get there a lot faster. Then he came on a sponge who persuaded him to part with the rest of his money in exchange for a jet propelled scooter so that he would be able to get there even faster. As he sped through the sea five times as fast he met a shark who, pointing into his large open mouth, suggested that this was a short cut to his fortune which would save a lot of time. The sea horse thanked him and zoomed into the interior of the shark, there to meet his destruction.

Mager was suggesting that some teachers are so keen to be progressive that they have forgotten to ask themselves where they are going. Within education the attitude to planning the content of instruction has ranged from the very rigid, where the teacher is almost told which page of what book he should be teaching, to the very free, where an individual teacher has complete freedom to do just what he likes. Not only do the external constraints on the teacher vary, indivual teachers may have widely differing views as to how explicitly aims and objectives should be stated. In America there is generally much more emphasis on stating very full objectives than there is in the United Kingdom. While a discussion of curriculum planning and control is beyond the scope of this book, it is obviously important for the teacher to be clear about the aims of each topic or lesson.

In most learning situations the teacher will employ a simple *instructional model* such as that proposed by Glaser (1962) and shown in figure 8.1.

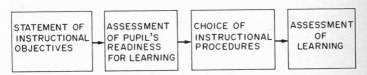

Figure 8.1 A simple instructional model (adapted from Glaser 1962)

Briefly, the statement of the instructional objectives requires a decision about what the pupils are to learn. The assessment of readiness for learning the new material involves choosing the starting point for the new learning in terms of what the pupil already knows and his level of cognitive development. The instructional procedures chosen will reflect the pupil's level of readiness as well as the content, sequence and method of presenting the material. Finally, a means of ascertaining what has been learned, and to what standard, is necessary to see whether the initial objectives have been reached. There are, of course, feedback loops between the stages, and the teacher will modify the instruction in the light of what he finds at each stage. For instance, if, after deciding on certain objectives, the teacher finds that the pupils have insufficient knowledge adequately to begin the topic, then the objectives will need to be amended.

TYPES OF EVALUATION

The employment of an instructional model aids the distinction between the various types of assessment that the teacher will use. Bloom, Hastings and Madaus (1971) claimed that the purpose of evaluation, as it is frequently used in the existing educational system, is primarily the grading and classifying of pupils. The end of term examinations in schools and colleges are usually of this type. They noted that testing, as it is commonly used in schools, contributes little to the improvement of teaching and learning. They saw assessment as important throughout all the stages of the instructional process, and distinguished three types of evaluation:

1 *Initial evaluation* of readiness for the new learning based on three sources; (a) the teacher's knowledge of the child's previous relevant achievement; (b) a determination of the pupil's existing knowledge that is necessary to the understanding of the learning; and (c) tests of aptitude and personality to aid the choice of learning approaches (e.g. discovery/reception, individual/group).

2 *Formative evaluation* during instruction by means of tests for each learning task, and on the basis of these the analysis and diagnosis of what must still be learned.

3 *Summative evaluation* to decide the extent to which the objectives have been achieved for an individual learner and for

the group.

It is not suggestedthat the teacher should necessarily formally test all of these stages on every occasion, but it is important that he should monitor performance throughout the learning of a topic to ensure that instruction is efficient.

THE COST OF EVALUATION

Since testing is time consuming both for the teacher and the pupil it is useful to consider the economics of evaluation. In doing this the teacher must take into account both the value of the decision and the type of decision that is to be made as a result of the testing.

Suppose you decide on certain objectives for the next learning unit for a group, you then face a decision concerning the evaluation of your pupils' readiness. As we have seen, readiness involves determining whether the learner has an adequate present knowledge of relevant information and a suitable level of cognitive development. Cronbach and Gleser (1970) considered testing from the standpoint of decision theory. They pointed out that in making a decision on the basis of a test we have to consider the cost of the final outcome. In the case we are considering as an example, we have to decide what level of readiness we will accept as adequate, and how rigorously we determine it in terms of the consequences of the outcome; in this case the new learning that is to take place.

When we have a pupil whose present knowledge seems to be a little deficient we have to decide whether we go ahead with the instruction, or whether we make up the deficiency. This decision must be made in terms of the costs involved. It may be that the objectives form the next step in a long chain of cumulative concepts, as in number work or learning a foreign language, in which case the omission of some key concept now may mean much trouble later. On the other hand, the concept missing from a readiness test may be peripheral and isolated, and one on which no great amount of future learning will depend. The amount of time spent testing and rectifying defects should be related to the cost of the decision.

A similar problem arises concerning the type of decision. Here we must ask what we expect of a test in relation to the decision we have to make. Suppose again that our test is one of readiness, and that we expect from past experience of our pupils that 75 per cent will pass the test, then we have to ask whether the test is of the right type for the job. Perhaps what we need is a short screening test to sift out the 25 per cent who are in difficulty. A long involved test for all the pupils would be wasteful. Having screened out the bottom 25 per cent we can then devote some of the saved time to more thorough diagnostic testing of the group that has difficulty.

THE VALIDITY OF ASSESSMENT

Cronbach (1970) listed three types of validity in testing: (1) content validity, do the tests truly sample *all* the content of the instruction, (2) educational importance, do tests measure an important educational outcome, and (3) construct validity, does the test measure what it is said to measure? It is the last of these three that the teacher is likely to find difficulty in deciding, and so the problems associated with it will now be considered.

Construct validity   When the teacher assesses, is he measuring what he hopes he is assessing? When he tests understanding, or comprehension, or learning, is he sure that it is in fact these constructs that he is evaluating? If he gives an intelligence test is he certain that he is actually measuring intelligence, or is he just hopefully assuming that he is?

The problem of making and choosing test items was demonstrated by Levy (1973). He described a study by Hopkins who considered one of the items of the Wechsler Intelligence Test. The item was the coding test which occurs in both the adult and children's version of the test. The item requires the subject to fill in the spaces beneath a series of twenty-five random digits with symbols given in a key. For instance the symbol, or code, for 'one' was a dash, for 'two' was a curved line like a bracket, for 'three' was a plus sign, and so on. The subject does the first seven digits as an example and is then instructed to work as quickly as he can. Two minutes are allowed for the coding test and the score is the number of digits that have been correctly coded in that time.

What would we expect this test to measure? Perhaps the reader would like to ponder this for a moment? I asked a remedial reading specialist this question. His view was that the test measured the ability to perceive spatial relationships. Hopkins attempted to discover what the test does in fact measure by retaining the basic form of the item and then systematically changing aspects of it using a group of thirteen-year-old children as subjects. He gave the subjects the test together with two modified versions of it. In the first modification subjects were simply required to fill in each space with a number 'five' to test writing speed. In the second version the subjects had to copy into the blank spaces either / or = which were printed randomly along the top of each line. This test was considered to be basically a measure of eye movement control since the subjects had to look at the symbol and then move their eyes down to copy the symbol in the space immediately beneath it, and then up again to note the next symbol to be drawn, and so on.

He found that the writing speed test performance correlated 0·47 with the score on the original coding test, indicating that part of what the test measured was writing ability. The second version of the item correlated 0·68 with the standard test, and when it is noted that the reliability of the coding test is only 0·81, it is seen that the coding item is principally a test of writing and eye movement abilities. If you thought that this was what the test was likely to measure, well done! It is unlikely that Wechsler did or he would not have included it in his test. The important point to notice is that tests do not always measure what they are claimed to measure, nor is exactly what they do measure necessarily self evident.

Validity of school assessment   Moving to testing within the school situation, a student teacher in an infants school taught and tested basic shapes in the following way.

'Here are some shapes (shows a green circle, blue square, red triangle), this is a circle, this is a square, and this is a triangle.' She continues this with further repetition and asks the children for the names as she points to the coloured shapes on a card. Later in the day she calls a child to her, holds up the card with the coloured shapes on and says, 'Now Johnny, tell me the name of this shape (she points to the red triangle); a triangle, yes, good, that is right'. I asked her whether she thought Johnny had the concept of triangularity. 'Of course', she replied, 'I have tested him, haven't I?' What does the reader think? The child may have learned the concept of a triangle as a three-sided figure, or he may erroneously think that any red shape is a triangle if he happened to pick on the wrong attribute as being the relevant one. To be sure that Johnny had the concept of triangularity the teacher would need him to consistently choose the triangle from other shapes with the colours changed, with the positions changed, size changed and orientation changed.

Or, thinking of the secondary level, a young science teacher enthused over the use of objective tests. 'After all,' he said, 'they test whether children really understand, don't they?' He showed me one of his test items. It was of the multiple choice type in which the pupil had to mark the answer that was the correct one: 'Pressure is defined as, (a) mass per unit volume, (b) force per unit area, (c) mass times acceleration.' 'If the pupil responds with (b) he obviously has the concept of pressure. . . .' What does the reader think? The pupil may have rotely learned some definitions without any real understanding of them.

A better test item would be an operational one. For instance, in terms of pressure, questions such as, why are snowshoes worn in arctic regions, why are football boot studs effective, how do ice skates grip; or, why does a sharp knife cut more readily than a blunt one, or, why is a ladder sometimes used to rescue someone who has fallen through thin ice in the middle of a pond? Such explanations would require the child to use his knowledge of pressure and to demonstrate that he understands it.

Operationalism Bloom, Hastings and Madaus (1971) pointed out that attempts to define constructs by giving synonyms of them are not really helpful. For instance, to say that intelligence is the 'sum of our mental abilities', or that 'comprehension' is 'understanding', does not help to measure the construct. Rather, constructs need to be defined in terms of observable behaviours or *operations*. If we employ a word like 'understanding', or 'appreciation', or even 'learning', when stating aims and objectives, then they are likely to be vague and difficult to communicate because different people will mean different things by these terms. They will also be hard to measure, or at least we shall be uncertain as to how to measure them.

On the other hand, if objectives are stated operationally, in terms of observable actions, then there is much less ambiguity. When given operationally they will contain verbs which describe what the pupil does to demonstrate that he has achieved the objective, for example, to state, to recognise, and to evaluate. For instance, to give as an objective 'To learn about area' is too vague, whereas to say 'To be able to calculate the area of a rectangle' is easier to test.

Bormuth (1970) took operationalism one step further, for he argued that not only should the objective be stated operationally in terms of what the pupil should be able to do after receiving the instruction, but also the test question should be related to, and derived from, the instruction by a set of operations or rules. Bormuth considered that if the science of testing is to advance, then there must be agreed rules as to how the test items are chosen and constructed, otherwise two testers given the same objectives and instructional content will finish up with two quite different tests, which might well produce very different results even if they are given to the same learners.

In practical terms, the teacher needs to consider the extent to which the aims and objectives for a topic can be expressed in observable actions that can be readily measured at the end of the instruction. He must be alert to the problems of deciding what a particular test actually measures, and, perhaps most difficult of all, he needs to be systematic in the way in which he constructs tests of learning performance.

INTERPRETING ASSESSMENT

There are two common mistakes that it is easy to make when interpreting test results. The first is to place more trust in the result than the accuracy of the test warrants. You go into a class and the teacher points out a child and says, 'She is bright, I.Q. of 136', and it is said with a finality that suggests 136·382, when in fact the accuracy is more likely to be 136±25.

The second error is to neglect the different distributions of test results when making a comparison between tests. Bowley (1967) quoted an amusing tale which nicely demonstrates this. The head of a secondary school had to award a prize to the best fourth form pupil. The marks of the eight end-of-term examination papers (maths, history, etc.) were totalled for each pupil. Apparently Smith, who had the highest total, would receive the prize. However, the head of the science department pointed out that the spread of the marks was not the same for each paper. So the head of the maths department scaled the scores and retotalled them. To everyone's amazement the form order was reversed, with Smith last and Samson, who had been last, now first! While in practice such a dramatic reversal is unlikely, it is important to scale scores when comparing performance on several tests.

Sequencing learning

In learning, both the order in which topics are to be considered, and the sequence of the material within each topic, must be determined. The aim here will be to look at the general principles of sequencing which may be applied to subject matter, rather than the order of a specific curriculum.

A basic problem for the teacher when considering the order in which a subject should be presented is that he cannot view the subject matter from the point of view of the learner. In fact, the more a teacher knows about a subject the harder it is, in some ways, to teach, because he is less able to predict which parts of the material are likely to be difficult to grasp. That learners often prefer to consider information in an order different from that expected by the teacher was shown by Mager (1961).

He allowed six adult subjects from widely varying educational backgrounds to independently learn some electronics from a teacher. The subjects had complete control over both what they learned and the order in which it was considered. The teacher was there to answer questions and to give instruction, examples and problems only as the subject requested them. Each subject had four learning sessions each lasting approximately one hour. It was found that, (1) the subjects tended to start with a topic different from that usually chosen by the teacher, (2) the sequences used by the subjects were broadly similar, and (3) the sequences chosen were not similar to those in common electronics courses. These findings emphasise the need for the teacher to carefully consider the order in which information should be learned by pupils. They warn against the teacher assuming that his idea of the best order of the subject matter, viewed from the position of having learned it, is perforce the best order for his pupils.

Decisions about the order of learning will be based on both the logical order of the content of the subject matter, and evidence about the best psychological order. It may be helpful to illustrate these two factors by considering the order in which basic number work, such as addition, subtraction, multiplication and division, might be learned. *Logically*, subtraction, or counting back, is an extension of addition and so should be learned immediately after addition. Multiplication, or repeated addition, is also an extension. Similarly, division is repeated subtraction. A reasonable logical order is therefore: addition, subtraction, multiplication and division.

However, the learning order may need to be modified because of *psychological evidence* about learning. The basic psychological principle of learning is that there should be within the learner's organised memory the necessary concepts to which the new information can be related. Since information in memory often becomes less available for recall with time, a learner may find that going from subtraction to multiplication causes problems in that some aspects of addition may have been forgotten, and so a revision session on addition will be necessary before proceeding to multiplication. Similarly, review of subtraction may also be needed prior to division.

Such an illustration demonstrates the two fundamental determiners of learning sequences, and these will be considered in more detail.

THE LOGICAL DETERMINATION OF SUBJECT MATTER ORDER

In absolute terms there is probably no final logical order for the subject matter in a topic, because different teachers will tend to view the material slightly differently, and their orders will reflect their own organisations of the material in memory. However, there is likely to be a fair degree of agreement among teachers concerning the main aspects of logical order. Several systems for helping the teacher to determine the logical sequencing of subject matter have been suggested. One of these is the system devised by Mechner (1961).

The system, basically, is to take the concept, or concepts, to be learned and to analyse them into subconcepts, and then into even more specific items of information. Suppose you wish to teach three major related concepts, A, B and C, in that order. Each concept is divided into its subconcepts, $A_1, A_2, A_3, \ldots A_n$; $B_1, B_2, B_3, \ldots B_n$, and $C_1, C_2, C_3, \ldots C_n$, and then each subconcept is divided again into $a_1, a_2, a_3, \ldots a_n$; $b_1, b_2, b_3, \ldots b_n$; $c_1, c_2, c_3, \ldots c_n$, until they are about the right size to teach. A tentative analysis of the concept of 'length', using this method, is given in figure 8.2. According to this approach, the teacher would start from the top right at the most specific level and proceed down the page. While this may give a reasonable logical sequence, it is likely that the order will need to be altered to take into account psychological evidence about the best learning order.

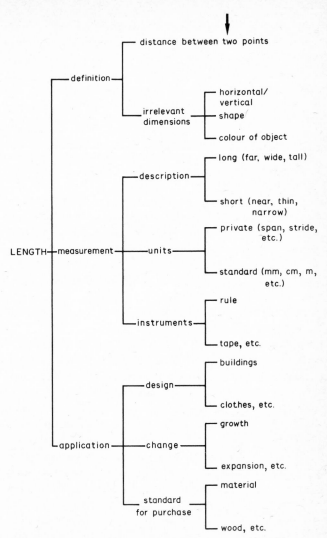

Figure 8.2 An analysis of the concept of 'length'

LEARNING SEQUENCE AND THE PUPIL'S KNOW-LEDGE

It has already been stressed that for learning to be efficient and meaningful, the new material must be relatable to what the pupil already knows.

For new learning to be efficient, then, three basic conditions concerning the pupil's present knowledge must be fulfilled:

1 The necessary relevant concepts to which the new material can be related must already be in the child's memory.

2 This relevant knowledge must be readily available for recall so that the new learning can proceed at a reasonable rate.

3 When the new information has been received into LTM, it should be accommodated fully into the structure of knowledge already stored.

These three conditions will tend to modify the logical order of the subject matter presentation, and so they will be considered in turn.

SEQUENCE AND COGNITIVE STRUCTURE

Ausubel (1968) has argued that for new learning to be meaningful it must be attached to what is already known to the pupil. If information is presented that is not relatable to existing concepts in LTM then, and it is learned at all, the learning will be rote and the new material stored as an isolated package. Rote learning takes longer than meaningful learning, and because the information is poorly organised in memory, retention is often poor.

Since this is an important point let's try a couple of simple examples. What do you make of the following words, 'dog', 'quagga'? Take 'dog' first. You found this word very meaningful because it is well organised in your LTM. It readily brought many associations. It evoked a visual image; it has associations with similar concepts like fox, wolf and, perhaps, cat; it has associations with instances within the conceptual category such as alsatian, poodle, collie; it has associations with more inclusive ideas like animal and mammal. Thus 'dog' readily produces many associations, and it is this variety of associations that makes the word meaningful for us. If we were to read a novel which made mention of a dog in the plot we would experience no difficulty in understanding it in a meaningful way. By contrast, if the tale featured a quagga it is likely that things would be different, because for most readers the term lacks meaning. That is, when we read the word we get no associations and the word is nonsense, and so we cannot link new information to it.

What would make the term 'quagga' meaningful? Well, if you are told that a quagga was an animal related to the donkey and the zebra, and that quaggas are now extinct but once lived in southern Africa, then this would make the word meaningful to some degree, because you are able to relate, or link, it to concepts like donkey, zebra, and Africa, which are already familiar to you.

In school, before commencing on a topic the teacher must determine the concepts that are necessary to make it meaningful to his pupils, and then ensure that they are already known. If they are absent they will need to be taught before embarking on the main topic, so that the new information can be efficiently received.

The teacher will plan the topic so that all new concepts can be attached to those that have preceded them. In this respect, sequencing the topic bears some resemblance to building a wall, where each course of bricks must be laid on the bricks already in position. If any bricks are missing from a course, the next course will not only be difficult to lay, but also unstable. Similarly with the understanding of a topic. If concepts are omitted or not learned, then other ideas that are dependent on them for meaning will be difficult to learn and store later. Generally, if the subject matter is logically sequenced, then it will conform to this requirement.

However, a problem can arise for the teacher where a cumulative subject, like mathematics, is taught over many years by several teachers. Poor planning, or lack of communication between teachers, or absences because of illness, can result in some of the important concepts necessary to future learning being absent from the pupil's LTM. In such cases the 'bricks' that are lacking will need to be replaced.

SEQUENCE AND THE AVAILABILITY OF INFORMATION IN MEMORY

While information may be in LTM it may not always be very available. The reader may have found that, when faced with a new area of study, or when working on material learned some time ago, it takes time to get into the material. It is as if the area of memory associated with the work requires to be aroused so that the information in it is more readily available. The implication of this need to 'warm up' is that if the concepts necessary for new material to be received are not aroused before the main learning session gets going, the reception may be inefficient. If a child is listening to a story, for instance, and the words he hears need to be pondered over, then he may lose the sense of some of the details.

Advance organisers   For learning to be effective the necessary relevant concepts must both be in memory and be readily available for recall. In order to ensure successful learning, Ausubel (1968, p. 136) has explored the possibility of putting the essential concepts for new learning into memory, or, if they are already there, of arousing them, in advance of the presentation of the main learning material. To accomplish this he has proposed the use of a specially designed introduction, or 'advance organiser' as he termed it. The organiser presents, or reviews, the concepts to which the new information will be linked and subsumed. Ausubel argued that these concepts should be more inclusive and general than the material to be learned, so that the new information can be readily subsumed into these anchorage points. He further suggested that the organisers will arouse and mobilise the relevant concepts the learner already has in memory. He concluded that the use of an organiser should make the learning in the main topic more meaningful. A number of studies have investigated the effectiveness of organisers.

The facilitating effect of an advance organiser compared with the more traditional introduction has been shown by Ausubel (1960) in teaching a topic on metallurgy. The scheme of the experiment is shown in figure 8.3. A control group read a traditional introduction typical of metallurgical textbooks, which gave historical material about iron and steel processing.

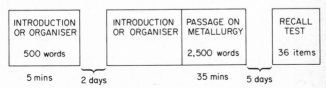

Figure 8.3 Comparison of organiser with introduction

The experimental group studied an organiser which dealt with metals and alloys. Both groups then received the passage on the properties of steel, followed five days later by a recall test. The essential difference between the organiser and the introduction was in conceptual content. The introduction did not contain concepts which could be used by the learner as subsumers for the information in the passage to be learned, while the advance organiser did. The organiser did not give information that would allow items on the final recall test to be answered. The mean recall scores were: experimental group 16.7, control group 14.1. The results suggest that the organiser was marginally more effective in aiding learning than the ordinary introduction.

Organiser effectiveness and the pupil's knowledge　In a study by Ausubel and Fitzgerald (1962) it was found that low verbal ability subjects benefited more from an organiser than those of high ability. On the other hand Grotelueschen and Sjorgen (1968) showed that organisers can be effective with adults of superior intelligence who have little prior knowledge of the learning topic.

Kuhn and Novak (1971) found that an advance organiser is effective when the learners are fairly unfamiliar with the subject matter. They compared the use of two types of introduction on the learning of material by university students taking an introductory biology course. One group received an organiser which dealt with the principles of homoeostasis and which gave background material for the main learning passage. The organiser was at a higher level of abstraction, generality and inclusiveness than the main passage. It was designed to provide structure and a subsuming framework for the main passage material.

A control group received an introductory passage which was historical in nature. It was not intended to supply a conceptual framework for the material in the main passage. Both introductions were 800 words long, and neither gave information which allowed items on the recall test to be answered. The scheme of the experiment is shown in figure 8.4.

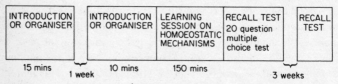

Figure 8.4 Organiser versus introduction in biology

A pre-test was given to all subjects before the experiment and this showed that the students knew very little about the material. The performance on the recall test is given in table 8.1. The students who recalled after three weeks had also recalled immediately.

Table 8.1   Recall scores for organiser and introduction groups
(adapted from Kuhn and Novak 1971)

Group	Mean recall test score after retention interval (weeks)	
	0	3
Advance organiser	12·2	10·2
Historical introduction	9·9	7·7

It is clear that the advance organiser produced better initial learning and that this superior level was maintained during the three week retention period. It seems probable, then, that the basic variable affecting the effectiveness of an advance organiser is the pupil's present knowledge of concepts relevant to the new learning. If he already has available the necessary concepts under which new information is to be subsumed, then little will be gained by using an organiser. This point will be discussed further later in the chapter.

For comprehensive reviews of the effect of the pupil's prior knowledge on the learning of science concepts the reader is referred to articles by Novak, Ring and Tamir (1971) and West and Fensham (1974).

The need for revision   The order in which information is presented will also be influenced by the need for periodic review of what has already been learned. In chapter 4 we saw that with time information is forgotten, but that with revision it may be maintained in memory. The precise intervals between review sessions will depend on the subject matter. In any case, in practice most learning is cumulative. A typical learning sequence of topics may be represented as follows: learn material A — recall A and learn related material B — recall AB and learn related information C — recall ABC and learn D — and so on. With this sort of sequence in mind Bruner (1960, p. 52) has suggested a *spiral curriculum* in which, periodically, new information is learned and added to a series of basic concepts. Consider three basic concepts or ideas which are denoted by A, B and C. A spiral sequence might be as shown diagrammatically in figure 8.5, in which developments, or additions, to the basic area are connected by broken lines, and the sequence of presentation is shown by a continuous line. A2, A3 and so on indicate the additions or extensions of the basic area of subject matter denoted by A1.

As a practical example, A, B and C might represent the three fundamental aspects of number work, the concepts of number, addition and subtraction. A1, 2 and 3 might then be extensions

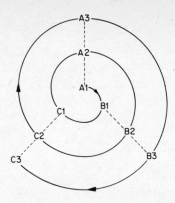

Figure 8.5 Schematic diagram of a spiral curriculum

of the basic concept and could deal with counting in tens and hundreds, fractions of whole numbers, decimals and so on. B1, 2 and 3 could be addition, simple multiplication, and long multiplication. C1, 2 and 3 could be simple subtraction, subtraction of tens and hundreds, and simple division.

A spiral arrangement of the subject matter has the advantage the periodic revision of each of the concept areas is undertaken.

SEQUENCE AND THE ACCOMMODATION OF INFORMATION INTO MEMORY

Ausubel (1968, p. 152) proposed two principles which he argued should aid the accommodation of information into the learner's memory structure. Before considering these a point made in chapter 3 may be noted. For learning to be complete, new information must not only be transferred to LTM but also be linked to the relevant related material already there. If it is accepted into LTM without being properly integrated into the structure, the new learning will be rote and the information will be stored in isolation from other items. The teacher should therefore make every effort to ensure that the pupil has the opportunity to accommodate new learning as fully as possible into what he already knows.

Sequence from the general to the specific   Ausubel's first principle is that, in learning a topic, the more inclusive and general ideas should be presented first and further material should be ordered in terms of its inclusiveness so that the most specific details are presented last. He termed this principle, *progressive differentiation*. The reason for proceeding from the inclusive to the specific is so that the new material may be received into, or subsumed by, the more inclusive information. This idea is made more clear by considering the analysis of the concept of length in figure 8.2. To teach this topic according to the principle of progressive differentiation one would begin with the left-hand column of the material, followed by the second column, and then the right-hand column containing the most specific concepts. (This will, in fact, give a spiral presentation.) At the highest and most inclusive level the general idea of 'length' would be introduced, followed at the next level by the explanation of how it is described, measured and the practical uses of the concept. At the next level each of these will be further expanded, and so on. The intention is that each level should act as a subsumer, or anchoring point, for the material in the next, and this should make the reception easier and more meaningful. Obviously, just how this is done, and the level of inclusiveness taken as the starting point, will depend both on the topic and the age of the children. With younger children the starting level will be much more specific than with older pupils.

The order of the subject matter according to progressive differentiation is often not the order of many school textbooks, particularly at the secondary level, in which the material is usually considered in the reverse order, that is from the specific to the general.

Evidence that sequencing material hierarchically improves learning comes indirectly from a second experiment on the use of organisers by Kuhn and Novak (1971). Students taking an introductory biology course received either an advance organiser or an historical introduction for the ten minutes immediately before a 150 minute main learning session on levels of biological organisation. Immediately after the main learning and again after three and six weeks, all subjects received a twenty-one item multiple choice recall test. The principal difference between this experiment and the one of theirs described earlier was that the main learning material was *hierarchically organised* (i.e. from the general to the specific) to aid its reception into memory by the students. The mean recall test scores are given in table 8.2.

Table 8.2 Recall scores for organiser and introduction

(adapted from Kuhn and Novak 1971)

Group	Mean recall test score after retention interval (weeks)		
	0	3	6
Advance organiser	16·4	12·2	12·1
Historical intro.	14·8	11·8	11·0

It is noted that compared to the non-hierarchically organised information used in the first experiment, the differences between the groups tend to be smaller, particularly after a few weeks. This suggests that material sequenced from the general to the specific is more readily learned, and that where information is structured in this way an advance organiser is less necessary.

What, then, is the merit of progressive differentiation as a basis for sequencing subject matter for instruction? Ausubel argued that if the natural and most efficient way of learning is to attach new information to a more inclusive concept, then since progressive differentiation allows this to happen, it commends itself as the best way of ordering information.

Integrative reconciliation   A second principle is that learning should be related as fully as possible to all the similar and relevant information already in the pupil's memory. Ausubel termed this principle *integrative reconciliation*. The aim is that when a new concept is learned, the student should be given opportunity to explore the relationships between this new information and the related structure so that links can be established and any inconsistencies resolved or noted. Ausubel pointed out that if the pupil is not encouraged to integrate and reconcile new material with established concepts in LTM, he may use several terms for one concept because he does not realise that they are really the same. In addition to making the structure of information unnecessarily complex and illogical, this tends to separate topics which are related in content or principle. This will then result in further learning being inefficient, because it will not be clear to the learner to which concepts in memory additional concepts should be attached.

The principle of integrative reconciliation again points to a spiral curriculum, since each time new work is introduced the links between it and similar concepts can be explored, as indicated by the broken lines in figure 8.5. A learning sequence designed to take into account the pupil's present knowledge and the most efficient method of accommodating new information into it, will quite extensively modify the logical order of the subject matter. Generally this modification will require changing a chain-like logical sequence into a spiral progression through the material. The progression will be from the inclusive to the general, allowing opportunities for review and exploration of relationships and differences, at periodic intervals. However, the construction of a good sequence for a topic is not easy and can be very time consuming. The reader may find it instructive to choose a topic and sequence it according to the principles.

Learning activities

The activities pupils undertake during the instruction may range from reading about the topic to expressing the information in their own words, or from looking at an illustration to making their own model or putting the material into dramatic form. In choosing activities the teacher must bear in mind the two basic reasons for employing them. The first is to ensure that learning is active and the second that the material is accommodated into memory. In chapter 2 it was pointed out that there is the danger that material may be only partially processed in STM with the consequence that it is not completely transferred to LTM and so not learned. Tasks done during learning will help the pupil to analyse information more fully. Further, information must not only be received into LTM, but also related to relevant subsuming concepts, if the learning is to be meaningful, stable and is to form a structure of knowledge. The learning activity can help the pupil to form such links and to consider the relationships between the new material and what he already knows.

A basic principle that emerges from experimental studies of learning and retention is that while the input of information is essential to its reception, the output of the material is basic to its accommodation. Many teachers will have found that it is not until they come to teach a topic that they realise the incompleteness of, and contradictions in, their own knowledge of it. Recalling and expressing information allows the pupil to consider the links between the material and related ideas. For this reason more effective learning and retention results from presentation of information followed by recall than from repeated presentation.

This principle has been demonstrated by several studies, although the learning material used was word lists rather than material more typical of school learning. Allen, Mahler and Estes (1969) visually presented university student subjects with a list of twenty-seven noun–number pairs. When tested after twenty-four hours the percentage of correct recall and the speed of recall was found to depend on the number of presentations. The results are given in table 8.3.

It is seen that doubling the number of presentations did, as might be expected, improve learning, but from the teacher's point of view, the interesting result is the effect of having five presentations followed by five attempts at recall. During these five recalls no knowledge of results was given. There was very little difference in initial learning between the two methods, but the presentation plus recall method resulted in much better

Table 8.3 Percentage of correct recall of number after word

(adapted from Allen, Mahler and Estes 1969)

Learning activity	Percentage recall associated number after retention interval (hours)		Mean response time in secs after 24 hours
	0	24	
5 presentations	83	58	2·6
10 presentations	93	65	2·5
5 presentations plus 5 recall tests	91	82	2·1

retention over twenty-four hours and also quicker recall.

The results suggest that a learning activity which includes recall or output of the information being learned, produces a memory structure for the material that is both easier to retrieve and more stable.

That the student does in fact find the information easier to locate in memory is demonstrated by a study by Hogan and Kintsch (1971), who compared the effect of learning activities on recall and recognition. In recognition the subject is prompted in his retrieval of information because he has only to decide whether he recognises that an item has occurred previously, whereas in recall he has to depend on the efficiency of his organisation of the information in memory to allow him to locate it.

They used four groups of university students. Two groups had four visual presentations of a forty-word list, while the remainder received only one presentation followed by three attempts at recall. After two days one group from each treatment was given a recall test while the others had a recognition test. The performance on the tests is given in table 8.4. It is clear that while output activity aids subsequent recall, it does not help recognition. The recognition scores were very much higher than those for recall. In most school learning the level of retention required is for recall and not recognition. Since recognition is fairly easy compared to recall, when pupils look through material which they think they know, they can be misled concernining their knowledge if they rely on recognition as a guide.

Table 8.4 Effect of learning activity on recognition and recall
(adapted from Hogan and Kintsch 1971)

Group	Learning activity	Mean test score
		Recall
A	4 presentations	6·1
B	1 presentation plus 3 recalls	8·2
		Recognition
C	4 presentations	33·6
D	1 presentation plus 3 recalls	26·8

Studies using prose material Studies using prose material typical of school learning have compared repetition with no repetition, and immediate recall with no immediate recall, but not the relative effects on retention of additional presentation and recall.

In an early study, Peterson, Ellis, Toohill and Kloess (1935) gave groups of undergraduates a twenty-five line passage on the origins of monasticism in Western Europe. Control groups read the passage followed by immediate free recall. Other groups, after the initial reading and recall, received in addition either one or two further opportunities to read and recall immediately after the first reading and recall. The percentage recall by the groups after six and eighteen weeks is given in table 8.5. A different group was used for each treatment and retention interval.

It is seen that recall after both six and eighteen weeks is directly proportional to the number of presentation-recalls because these activities resulted in better consolidated learning. In view of the findings of the studies using word lists it is likely that the recall part of the activity rather than additional presentations was responsible for the improved quality of the learning.

The consolidating effect of immediate recall alone was demonstrated by Spitzer (1939), who gave eleven-year-old

Table 8.5 Recall of passage after different activities

(adapted from Peterson and others 1935)

No of presentation-recalls at initial learning session	Percentage of detail free-recalled after retention interval (weeks)	
	6	18
1	32	29
2	40	35
3	55	44

children eight minutes to study a 600 word passage about bamboo plants. One group of children were tested immediately and then after one week, while another had no immediate recall. The percentage recall scores at the end of the week were, respectively, 48 and 32.

School learning activities The basic principle, then, is that successful learning results from a combination of input and output. In school, activities that are frequently used include working out problems, expressing material in the child's own words, producing a picture or model to depict information and acting out events. All of these require the pupil to apply or express what he has in memory. Obviously the type of activity will depend on the subject matter and the age of the learner. Ten-year-olds doing a topic on the Tudor period might write about what they have heard, draw pictures depicting everyday life, make models of buildings and perhaps act out some notable historic event of the period. Secondary pupils learning to solve equations in mathematics might be asked to explain the principles of finding the unknown term and required to work through a series of problems so that they can apply the method.

It is important to note that, to be effective, the learning activity must involve the LTM material. An activity such as copying a paragraph from a book, or, to a lesser extent, a picture, will probably not force the pupil to consider the links between the new material and what he already knows.

PLANNING SCHOOL LEARNING

Learning in school will be efficient only if the teacher is aware of what learning he hopes will take place and has means of measuring or evaluating the final performance. Unclear aims on the part of the teacher will result in poor attainment on the part of the children.

In deciding on the starting point for new learning the teacher will need to take careful account of what the children already know and to begin from there.

We have seen that the learner tends to view the order in which he wants to learn a subject rather differently from the order suggested by the teacher, who is an expert in that area. The reason for this is probably that once a person has acquired a good knowledge of an area he tends to look at the subject matter in its logical entirety rather than in terms of the actual difficulties of initially learning it. While the logical order of the material may form the basis for the order in which it is learned, the learner's memory structure, the need for review and the importance of including learning activities will mean that the logical order will need to be quite substantially modified if instruction is to be efficient.

In planning learning activities the basic principle is that the optimum results are likely to result from a combination of both input of information and output in terms of self-expression by the learner.

TO THINK ABOUT

1 What are the values, and the limitations, of precisely stating the objectives for an intended piece of instruction?

2 To what extent do you agree with Bloom and others (1971) that there is too little of the right sort of evaluation in school? What testing programme would you like to see in a given school?

3 Assess the importance of operationalism in test construction.

4 Design, in outline, an advance organiser suitable for a specific topic, age range and ability.

5 What advantages are there in sequencing material for learning according to the principle of progressive differentiation? In note form plan a topic in this manner.

6 Briefly describe some learning activities and state which part of the reception-accommodation process they are likely to facilitate.

References and Name index

The numbers in italics following each entry are page references to discussions of authors within this book.

The following abbreviations are used:
JVLVB *Journal of Verbal Learning and Verbal Behavior*
JEP *Journal of Educational Psychology*

ALLEN, G. A., MAHLER, W. A. and ESTES, W. K. (1969) 'Effects of Recall Tests on Long-term Retention of Paired Associates', *JVLVB* **8**, 463-70. *152*

AUSUBEL, D. P. (1960) 'The Use of Advance Organizers in the Learning and Retention of Meaningful Verbal Material', *JEP* **51**, 267-72. *145*

AUSUBEL, D. P. (1968) *Educational Psychology: A Cognitive View* (New York: Holt, Rinehart and Winston). *26, 42, 60, 88, 104, 142, 144*

AUSUBEL, D. P. and FITZGERALD, D. (1962) 'Organiser, General Background and Antecedent Learning Variables in Sequential Verbal Learning', *JEP* **53**, 243-9. *145*

AUSUBEL, D. P., STAGER, M. and GAITE, A. J. H. (1968) 'Retroactive Facilitation in Meaningful Verbal Learning', *JEP* **59**, 250-5. *83*

BACH, M. J. and UNDERWOOD, B. J. (1970) 'Developmental Changes in Memory Attributes', *JEP* **61**, 292-6. *37*

BARTLETT, F. C. (1932) *Remembering* (Cambridge: Cambridge University Press). *25, 35, 89*

BIRCH, H. G. and RABINOWITZ, H. S. (1951) 'The Negative Effect of Previous Experience on Productive Thinking', *Journal of Experimental Psychology* **41**, 121-5. *97*

BLOOM, B. S., HASTINGS, J. T. AND MADAUS, G. F. (1971) *Handbook of Formative and Summative Evaluation of Student Learning* (New York: McGraw-Hill). *132, 137*

BORMUTH, J. R. (1970) *On the Theory of Achievement Test Items* (Chicago, Ill.: University of Chicago Press). *137*

BOURNE, L. E. and O'BANION, K. (1971) 'Conceptual Rule Learning and Chronological Age', *Developmental Psychology* **5**, 525-34. *55*

BOUSFIELD, W. A. (1953) 'The Occurrence of Clustering in the Recall of Randomly Arranged Associates', *Journal of General Psychology* **49**, 229-40. *56, 91*

BOWER, G. H. and SPRINGSTONE, F. (1970) 'Pauses as Recoding Points in Letter Series', *Journal of Experimental Psychology* **83**, 421-30. *33*

BOWLEY, R. L. (1967) *Teaching without Tears* (London: Centaur Press). *138*

BRANSFORD, J. D., BARCLAY, J. R. and FRANKS, J. J. (1972) 'Sentence Memory: A Constructive versus Interpretive Approach', *Cognitive Psychology* **3**, 193-209. *35*

BRUNER, J. S. (1960) *The Process of Education* (Cambridge, Mass.: Harvard University Press). *147*

BRUNER, J. S. (1961) 'The Act of Discovery', *Harvard Educational Review* **31**, 21-32. *104*

CALVIN, A. D. (1962) 'Social Reinforcement', *Journal of Social Psychology* **66**, 15-19. *66*

CHAPIN, P. G., SMITH, T. S. and ABRAHAMSON, A. A. (1972) 'Two Factors in the Perceptual Segmentation of Speech', *JVLVB* **11**, 164-73. *32*

CHOMSKY, N. (1957) *Syntactic Structures* (The Hague: Mouton). *28*

CHOMSKY, N. (1965) *Aspects of the Theory of Syntax* (Cambridge, Mass.: Massachusetts Institute of Technology Press). *30*

COLLINS, A. M. and QUILLIAN, M. R. (1969) 'Retrieval Time from Semantic Memory', *JVLVB* **8**, 240-7. *57*

CONRY, J. (1976) Individual Differences in the Long-term Memory of Children, DCP thesis, Birmingham University. *85*

CORTIS, G. (1977) *The Social Context of Teaching* (London: Open Books). *62*

CRAIK, F. I. M. and LOCKHART, R. S. (1972) 'Levels of Processing: A Framework for Memory Research', *JVLVB* **11**, 671-84. *21*

CRONBACH, L. J. (1970) *Essentials of Psychological Testing*, 3rd ed. (New York: Harper and Row). *134*

CRONBACH, L. J. and GLESER, G. C. (1970) *Psychological Tests and Personnel Decisions* (Urbana, Ill.: Illinois University Press). *133*

CUNNINGHAM, J. D. (1965) 'Einstellung Rigidity in Children', *Journal of Experimental Child Psychology* **2**, 237-47. *99*

DARWIN, C. J., TURVEY, M. T. and CROWDER, R. G. (1972) 'An Auditory Analogue of the Sperling Partial Report Procedure', *Cognitive Psychology* **3**, 255-67. *11*

DOOLING, D. J. (1972) 'Some Context Effects in the Speeded Comprehension of Sentences', *Journal of Experimental Psychology*

93, 56-62. *34*

DUNCKER, K. (1945) 'On Problem Solving', *Psychological Monographs* **58**, no 270. *95*

ELLIOTT, C. D. (1972) 'Personality Factors and Scholastic Attainment', *British Journal of Educational Psychology* **42**, 23-32. *113*

ENTWISTLE, N. J. (1972) 'Personality and Academic Attainment', *British Journal of Educational Psychology* **42**, 137-51. *116*

EPSTEIN, W. (1969) 'Recall of Word Lists following Learning of Sentences and Anomalous and Random Strings', *JVLVB* **8**, 20-5. *30*

ERNEST, C. H. and PAIVIO, A. (1971) 'Imagery and Verbal Association Latencies as a Function of Imagery Ability', *Canadian Journal of Psychology* **25**, 83-90. *123*

EYSENCK, H. J. (1960) *The Structure of Human Personality* (London: University of London Press). *112*

EYSENCK, H. J. and COOKSON, D. (1969) 'Personality in Primary School Children: 1 Ability and Achievement', *British Journal of Educational Psychology* **39**, 109-22. *113*

EYSENCK, H. J. and HOWARTH, E. (1968) 'Extraversion, Arousal and Paired-associate Recall', *Journal of Experimental Research in Personality* **3**, 114-16. *118*

EYSENCK, H. J. and EYSENCK, S. B. G. (1964) *Eysenck Personality Inventory* (London: University of London Press). *112*

EYSENCK, S. B. G. (1965) *Junior Eysenck Personality Inventory* (London: University of London Press). *112*

FILE, S. E. and JEW, A. (1973) 'Syntax and the Recall of Instructions', *British Journal of Psychology* **64**, 65-70. *30*

FODOR, J. and BEVER, T. G. (1965) 'The Psychological Reality of Linguistic Segments', *JVLVB* **4**, 414-20. *31*

GAGNÉ, R. M. (1970) *The Conditions of Learning*, 2nd ed. (New York: Holt, Rinehart and Winston). *58*

GLANZER, M., GIANUTSOS, R. and DUBIN, S. (1969) 'The Removal of Items from Short-term Storage', *JVLVB* **8**, 435-47. *32*

GLASER, R. (1962) *Training Research and Education* (Pittsburgh: Pittsburgh University Press). *131*

GOLDMAN-EISLER, F. and COHEN, M. (1970) 'Is N, P and PN Difficulty a Valid Criterion of Transformational Operations'. *JVLVB* **9**, 161-6. *30*

GREGG, V. (1974) *Human Memory* (London: Methuen). *58*

GROTELUESCHEN, A. and SJORGEN, D. D. (1968) 'Effects of Differentially Structured Introductory Materials and Learning Tasks on Learning and Transfer', *American Educational Research Journal* **5**, 191-202. *145*

GUMMERMAN, K. and GRAY, C. R. (1972) 'Age, Iconic Storage and Visual Information Processing', *Journal of Experimental Child*

Psychology **13**, 165-70. *11*

HARRIS, G. J. and BURKE, B. (1972) 'The Effects of Grouping on Short-term Serial Recall of Digits by Children: Developmental Trends', *Child Development* **43**, 710-16. *37*

HARTER, S. (1974) 'Pleasure Derived by Children from Cognitive Challenge and Mastery', *Child Development* **45**, 661-9. *100*

HERMAN, G. (1969) 'Learning by Discovery: A Critical Review of Studies', *Journal of Experimental Education* **38**, 58-72. *110*

HERRIOT, P. (1970) *An Introduction to the Psychology of Language* (London: Methuen). *28*

HIGGINS, S. J. (1974) 'To Determine the Speed with which Children Process Information', DCP thesis, Birmingham University. *23*

HOCKEY, R. (1973) 'Rate of Presentation in Running Memory and Direct Manipulation of Input-processing Strategies', *Quarterly Journal of Experimental Psychology* **24**, 104-11. *36*

HOGAN, R. M. and KINTSCH, W. (1971) 'Differential Effects of Study and Test Trials on Long-term Recognition and Recall', *JVLVB* **10**, 562-7. *153*

HOLLENBERG, C. K. (1970) 'Functions of Visual Imagery in the Learning and Concept Formation of Children', *Child Development* **41**, 1003-15. *122*

HOWARTH, E. and EYSENCK, H. J. (1968) 'Extraversion, Arousal and Paired-associate Recall', *Journal of Experimental Research in Personality* **3**, 114-16. *118*

HOWE, E. S. (1970) 'Transformation, Associative Uncertainty and Free Recall of Sentences', *JVLVB* **9**, 425-31. *30*

HUCKABEE, M. W. (1974) 'Introversion–Extraversion and Imagery', *Psychological Reports* **34**, 453-4. *126*

HUNT, E. (1971) 'What Kind of Computer is Man?', *Cognitive Psychology* **2**, 57-98. *12*

JENKINS, J. B. and DALLENBACH, K. M. (1924) 'Obliviscience During Sleep and Waking', *American Journal of Psychology* **35**, 605-12. *86*

JONES, A. G. (1976) 'Personality and Memory in Children', M.Ed. thesis, Birmingham University. *119*

KALBAUGH, G. L. and WALLS, R. T. (1973) 'Retroactive and Proactive Interference in Prose Learning of Biographical and Science Materials, *JEP* **65**, 244-51. *83*

KERSH, B. Y. (1962) 'The Motivating Effect of Learning by Directed Discovery', *JEP* **53**, 65-71. *107*

KINSBOURNE, M. and COHEN, V. (1971) 'English and Hebrew Consonant Memory Span Related to the Structure of Written Language', *Acta Psychologica* **35**, 347-51. *38*

KUHN, D. J. and NOVAK, J. D. (1971) 'A Study of Cognitive

Subsumption in the Life Sciences', *Science Education* **55**, 309-20. *145, 149*

LEITH, G. O. M. (1973) 'The Effects of Extraversion and Methods of Programmed Instruction on Achievement', *Educational Research* **15**, 150-3. *118*

LEITH, G. O. M. and BOSSETT, R. (1967) 'Mode of Learning and Personality', Birmingham University Research Report on Programmed Learning, No 14. *120*

LEITH, G. O. M. and DAVIS, T. N. (1972) 'Age Changes in the Relation between Neuroticism and Achievement', *Research in Education* **8**, 61-70. *115*

LEITH, G. O. M. and TROWN, E. A. (1970) 'Influence of Personality and Task Conditions on Learning and Transfer', *Programmed Learning* **7**, 181-8. *117*

LEVY, P. M. (1973) 'On the Relation between Test Theory and Psychology', in P. Kline (ed.) *New Approaches in Psychological Measurement* (London: Wiley). *134*

LUCHINS, A. S. (1942) 'Mechanisation in Problem Solving', *Psychological Monographs* **54**, no 248, 1-95. *98*

MCCARVER, R. B. (1972) 'A Developmental Study of the Effect of Organizational cues on Short-term Memory', *Child Development* **43**, 1317-25. *37*

MCGEOCH, J. A. and MCDONALD, W. T. (1931) 'Meaningful Retention and Retractive Inhibition', *American Journal of Psychology* **43**, 579-88. *87*

MCMURRAY, D. W. and DUFFY, T. M. (1972) 'Meaningfulness and Pronounceability as Chunking Units in Short-term Memory', *Journal of Experimental Psychology* **96**, 291-6. *23*

MAGER, R. F. (1961) 'On the Sequencing of Instructional Content', *Psychological Reports* **9**, 405-13. *139*

MAGER, R. F. (1970) *Preparing Instructional Objectives* (Palo Alto, Calif.: Fearon Publishers). *130*

MARKS, D. F. (1973) 'Visual Imagery Differences in the Recall of Pictures', *British Journal of Psychology* **64**, 17-24. *122*

MECHNER, F. (1961) *Programming for Automated Instruction*, vol. 3 (New York: Basic Systems Inc.) *140*

MECONI, L. J. (1967) 'Concept Learning and Retention in Mathematics', *Journal of Experimental Education* **36**, 51-7. *108*

MEHLER, J. (1963) 'Some Effects of Grammatical Transformation on the Recall of English Sentences', *JVLVB* **2**, 346-51. *29*

MILLER, G. A. (1956) 'The Magical Number Seven, Plus-or-Minus Two: Some Limits on our Capacity for Processing Information', *Psychological Review* **63**, 81-97. *41*

MILLER, G. A. (1962) 'Some Psychological Studies of Grammar,

American Psychologist **17**, 748-62. *29*

MILLER, G. A., GALANTER, E. and PRIBRAM, K. H. (1960) *Plans and the Structure of Behavior* (New York: Holt). *98*

MILNER, B. (1970) 'Memory and Medial Temporal Regions of the Brain', in K. H. Pribram and D. E. Broadbent (eds) *Biology of Memory* (New York: Academic Press). *13*

MOSS, S. M. and SHARAC, J. (1970) 'Accuracy and Latency in Short-term Memory: Evidence for a Dual Retrieval Process', *Journal of Experimental Psychology* **84**, 40-6. *15*

NEISSER, U. (1967) *Cognitive Psychology* (New York: Appleton-Century-Crofts). *14*

NEWMAN, E. B. (1939) 'Forgetting of Meaningful Material during Sleep and Waking', *American Journal of Psychology* **52**, 65-71. *88*

NOVAK, J. D., RING, D. G. and TAMIR, P. (1971) 'Interpretation of Research Findings in Terms of Ausubel's Theory and Science Education', *Science Education* **55**, 483-526. *147*

O'CONNELL, D. C., TURNER, E. A. and ONUSKA, L. A. (1968) 'Intonation, Grammatical Structure, and Contextual Association in Immediate Recall', *JVLVB* **7**, 110-16. *34*

OSLER, S. F. and KOFSKY, E. (1965) 'Stimulus Uncertainty as a Variable in the Development of Conceptual Ability', *Journal of Experimental Child Psychology* **2**, 264-79. *52*

PAIVIO, A. (1971) *Imagery and Verbal Processes* (New York: Holt, Rinehart and Winston). *30*

PAIVIO, A. (1975) 'Imagery and Long-term Memory', in A. Kennedy and A. L. Wilkes (eds), *Studies in Long-term Memory* (London: Wiley). *89*

PETERSON, H. A., ELLIS, M., TOOHILL, N. and KLOESS, P. (1935) 'Some Measurements of the Effects of Reviews', *JEP* **26**, 65-72. *155*

PIAGET, J. (1950) *The Psychology of Intelligence* (New York: Harcourt Brace and World). *25*

POLLACK, R. H., PTASHNE, R. I. and CARTER, D. J. (1969) 'The Effects of Age and Intelligence on the Dark-interval Threshold', *Perception and Psychophysics* **6**, 50-2. *10*

RAY, W. E. (1961) 'Pupil Discovery versus Direct Instruction', *Journal of Experimental Education* **29**, 271-80. *105*

RIDING, R. J. (1975) 'A Method for Investigating the Perceptual Segmentation of Speech', *Language and Speech* **18**, 153-7. *32*

RIDING, R. J. and SHORE, J. M. (1974) 'A Comparison of Two Methods of Improving Prose Comprehension in Educationally Subnormal Children', *British Journal of Educational Psychology* **44**, 300-3. *19*

RIDING, R. J. and TAYLOR, E. M. (1976) 'Imagery Performance and Prose Comprehension in Seven Year Old Children', *Educational*

Studies **2**, 21-7. *124*

ROHRMAN, N. L. (1968) 'The Role of Syntactic Structure in the Recall of English Nominalisations', *JVLVB* **7**, 904-12. *30*

ROWELL, J. A., SIMON, J. and WISEMAN, R. (1969) 'Verbal Reception, Guided Discovery and the Learning of Schemata', *British Journal of Educational Psychology* **39**, 233-44. *108*

SAUGSTAAD, P. and RAAHEIM, K. (1960) Problem Solving, Past Experience and Availability of Function', *British Journal of Psychology* **51**, 97-104. *95*

SAVAGE, R. D. (1966) Personality factors and academic attainment in junior school children. *British Journal of Educational Psychology*, **34**, 91-2. *113*

SAVIN, H. B. and PERCHONOCK, E. (1965) 'Grammatical Structure and Immediate Recall of English Sentences', *JVLVB* **4**, 348-53. *29*

SAWYER, C. E. (1974) 'Reminiscence, Recall Order and Retention of Essential and Non-essential Details of Prose by Children', M.Ed. thesis, University of Birmingham. *75, 79*

SCHVANEVELAT, R. W. (1966) 'Concept Identification as a Function of Probability of Positive Instances and Number of Relevant Dimensions', *Journal of Experimental Psychology* **72**, 649-60. *52*

SCHWARTZ, D., SPARKMAN, J. P. and DEESE, J. (1970) 'The Process of Understanding and Judgments of Comprehensibility', *JVLVB* **9**, 87-93. *40*

SHUELL, T. J. and KEPPEL, G. (1970) 'Learning Ability and Retention', *JEP* **61**, 59-65. *84*

SKINNER, B. F. (1953) *Science and Human Behavior* (New York: Macmillan). *64*

SONES, A. M. and STROUD, J. B. (1940) 'Review with Special Reference to Temporal Position', *JEP* **31**, 665-76. *81*

SPERLING, G. (1960) 'The Information Available in Brief Visual Presentation', *Psychological Monographs* **74**, no 498. *10*

SPITZER, H. F. (1939) 'Studies in Retention', *JEP* **30**, 641-56. *154*

STRATTON, R. P. and BROWN, R. (1972) 'Improving Creative Thinking by Training in the Production and/or Judgment of Solutions', *JEP* **63**, 390-7. *101*

TALLMADGE, G. K. and SHEARER, J. W. (1971) 'Interactive Relationships among Learner Characteristics, Types of Learning, Instructional Methods, and Subject Matter Variables', *JEP* **62**, 31-8. *120*

TULVING, E. and ARBUCKLE, T. Y. (1963) 'Sources of Intratrial Interference in the Immediate Recall of Paired Associates', *JVLVB* **1**, 321-34. *15*

VINCENT, D. (1974) 'Phonetic, Syntactic and Semantic Coding in the Reception of Speech by Children', DCP thesis, Birmingham

University. *24, 41*

WARREN, R. E. (1972) 'Stimulus Encoding and Memory', *Journal of Experimental Psychology* **94**, 90-100. *38*

WEST, L. H. T. and FENSHAM, D. J. (1974) 'Prior Knowledge and the Learning of Science: A Review of Ausubel's Theory of this Process', *Studies in Science Education* **1**, 61-81. *147*

WITKIN, H. A. (1962) *Psychological Differentiation: Studies of Development* (New York: Wiley). *127*

WOODCOCK, R. M. and CLARK, C. (1968) 'Comprehension of a Narrative Passage by Elementary School Children as a Function of Listening Rate, Retention Period and I.Q.', *Journal of Communication* **18**, 259-71. *18*

Subject index